Remaking The International Monetary System

The Rio Agreement and Beyond

FRITZ MACHLUP is Walker Professor of Economics and International Finance and Director of the International Finance Section at Princeton University. Originally from Austria, he received his doctorate from the University of Vienna in 1923. He came to the United States in 1933 and was naturalized in 1940. From 1935 to 1947, he was Goodyear Professor of Economics at the University of Buffalo and then, Hutzler Professor of Political Economy at The Johns Hopkins University. From there, in 1960, he went to Princeton. He has been Visiting Lecturer at Harvard University and Visiting Professor at Cornell and American Universities and, in 1955, at Kyoto University and Doshisha University in Japan. Active in a number of professional organizations, he has served as President of the American Economic Association (1966) and of the American Association of University Professors (1962-64). He is a Fellow of the American Academy of Arts and Sciences and the American Association for the Advancement of Science and has been elected a member of the American Philosophical Society and the National Academy of Education. Professor Machlup is the author of numerous articles which have appeared in scholarly journals. Some of his more recent books include *International Payments, Debts, and Gold; Essays in Economic Semantics; The Political Economy of Monopoly;* and *The Economics of Seller's Competition.*

Fritz Machlup

Remaking The International Monetary System

The Rio Agreement and Beyond

June 1968

Supplementary Paper No. 24 issued by the
COMMITTEE FOR ECONOMIC DEVELOPMENT

Original Printing, June 1968

Library of Congress Catalog Card Number: 68-31419
Manufactured in the United States of America

332.152
M 184n

47852

A CED SUPPLEMENTARY PAPER

This Supplementary Paper is issued by the Research and Policy Committee of the Committee for Economic Development in conformity with the CED Bylaws (Art. V, Sec. 6), which authorize the publication of a manuscript as a Supplementary Paper if:

a) It is recommended for publication by the Project Director of a subcommittee because in his opinion, it "constitutes an important contribution to the understanding of a problem on which research has been initiated by the Research and Policy Committee" and,

b) It is approved for publication by a majority of an Editorial Board on the ground that it presents "an analysis which is a significant contribution to the understanding of the problem in question."

This Supplementary Paper relates to the Statement on National Policy, *The Dollar and the World Monetary System,* issued by the CED Research and Policy Committee in December 1966.

The members of the Editorial Board authorizing publication of this Supplementary Paper are:

While publication of this Supplementary Paper is authorized by CED's Bylaws, except as noted above its contents have not been approved, disapproved, or acted upon by the Committee for Economic Development, the Board of Trustees, the Research and Policy Committee, the Research Advisory Board, the Research Staff, or any member of any board or committee, or any officer of the Committee for Economic Development.

RESEARCH ADVISORY BOARD

Contents

Foreword

The structure and functioning of the international monetary and payments system has for a number of years presented problems which the Committee for Economic Development has regarded as extremely important. Recent months have recorded a succession of highly significant developments, among them the devaluation of the pound sterling, large-scale speculation in gold, and the decision of major governments not to buy or sell gold in private markets. These and other events, together with the persistent and apparently worsening deficit in the United States balance of payments, have placed world monetary problems in a new and critical context, increasing the urgency of taking effective national and international measures for their solution.

A very encouraging development has been the positive steps taken toward creation of "special drawing rights" in the International Monetary Fund. These SDR's are intended to serve as a new form of central bank reserve asset to meet the growing need for international liquidity. The historical background, the true nature of the SDR's, and the prospects for their successful establishment and use are the major concerns of the following lucid and interesting paper.

The author of the paper, Fritz Machlup, is an associate member of the CED Research Advisory Board. Professor Machlup has the highest of qualifications for writing in this field. His distinguished career is briefly summarized in the accompanying biographical statement.

The paper deals not only with the special drawing rights but also with the broader question of the characteristics of liquidity, adjustment, and confidence that an international monetary system must have to serve the requirements of today's world. These are all subjects which were dealt with at some length in a CED Policy Statement of

December 1966, *The Dollar and the World Monetary System*. Professor Machlup's paper shows in what respects the present system lacks these characteristics, and what alternative methods are available to remedy the defects. The author compares and evaluates these alternative methods and indicates his own preferences, not hesitating to suggest courses of action that some other specialists in the field have deemed to be either unnecessary, undesirable, or impossible of attainment.

The field of international monetary policy is a highly complex and controversial one for both theorists and practitioners. In publishing this paper the CED does not imply concurrence either with its proposals or with all aspects of the analysis. It is our belief, however, that so brilliant and timely a study of such an important problem ought to have a wide circulation among the readers of CED publications as well as other students of the problem. We are grateful to Professor Machlup for having written it and for his willingness to have it issued by CED as a Supplementary Paper.

HOWARD C. PETERSEN, *Chairman*
CED International Studies Subcommittee

Remaking the International Monetary System: The Rio Agreement and Beyond

Introduction

In olden times, authors of scholarly books as well as political pamphleteers could indulge in giving long and chatty titles to their literary products, titles and subtitles that extended over many lines and advertised several themes or theses sounded in their work. Had I exercised this now outmoded privilege, I would have chosen for my essay a subtitle reading like this:

Or, How to Get Agreement by Avoiding Excessively Clear Language

For, as I will undertake to show in the second part of this essay, the Rio Agreement on a new international monetary "facility" owes its existence to a linguistic pragmatism that proscribes the offensive practice of calling a spade a spade.

Preceding this story will be, as Part 1, a brief account of the international discussions that took place over a period of four years, beginning in September 1963 and reaching their conclusion in September 1967 with a resolution unanimously adopted by the Board of Governors of the International Monetary Fund (IMF) at their Annual Meeting, in Rio de Janeiro. The IMF Governors were the representatives of 107 member countries.

The third part of the essay will offer a concise description of the monetary scheme adopted in Rio. In order to be well understood, it will be necessary for me to go beyond the terminology used in the official document. After all, I want to be as clear as possible, even if this involves ruffling the feathers of some of my official readers.

The fourth part of my essay will be devoted to a discussion of the background and the implications of the new system. Alternative schemes that were considered but rejected by the negotiating parties will be compared with what was actually adopted in Rio. I shall also examine the consequences which the operation of the new system may have for various kinds of countries in different situations.

The fifth part will furnish semantic and theoretic explanations for the divergent interpretations of the agreement. There it will become clear why the avoidance of "excessively clear language" in the Agreement need not be a hindrance in the practical operation of the agreed scheme.

The sixth and concluding part will be chiefly a reminder of the fact that the Rio Agreement can solve, at best, *one* of the international monetary problems that are in need of solution. Other problems remain and will continue to challenge the imagination and, even more, the courage of the authorities.

The "Outline" of the Rio Agreement will be reproduced in Appendix A of this essay. Other appendices will supply a list of the titles of the (old and new) Articles of Agreement, a brief description of the proposed modifications of some of the old articles, the text of the twelve new articles drafted for ratification, and a lengthy statistical table. The amended and newly drafted Articles of Agreement were prepared pursuant to the Rio Agreement and became known only after this essay was completed and printed.

1.

Preliminary International Discussions

It was at the Annual Meeting of the International Monetary Fund in September 1961, held in Vienna, that the official experts recognized for the first time that not all was well and sound with the international monetary system. But the recognition went no further than to give assent to a proposal for "new borrowing arrangements . . . designed to provide the Fund with additional resources" needed to cope with unusually large movements of short-term capital.[1]

Such arrangements were agreed upon by ten industrial countries — Belgium, France, Germany, Italy, the Netherlands; Sweden, Canada, Japan; the United Kingdom and the United States — at a meeting in Paris in December 1961. This was the beginning of the Group of Ten, which later became the focal point of international monetary negotiations.

At the Annual Meeting of the Fund in September 1963, held in Washington, there was official recognition of the possibility that there might be more serious problems to be looked into. Two studies on "the outlook for the functioning of the international monetary system" were commissioned. One of the studies was to be made by the Group of Ten, the other by the International Monetary Fund.

The findings of both these studies were published in August 1964 and submitted to the Annual Meeting of the Fund, held in September of that year in Tokyo. The report on the study by the Fund was included in its *1964 Annual Report* as Chapters 3 and 4.

---

[1] International Monetary Fund, Press Release, January 8, 1962.

The findings of the Group of Ten appeared as a *Ministerial Statement*, issued by the "Ministers and Governors" of the ten countries, with an "Annex Prepared by Deputies." These Deputies of the Ministers and Governors had carried out their studies in cooperation with staff representatives of the Fund, the Organization for Economic Cooperation and Development (OECD), and the Bank for International Settlements (BIS), as well as an observer of the Swiss National Bank.

Both statements acknowledged that the time might come when more international liquidity would be needed than could be met by the supply of gold and foreign-exchange reserves. The *Ministerial Statement* declared that "This need may be met by an expansion of credit facilities and, in the longer run, may possibly call for some new form of reserve asset." The Ministers approved the establishment of "a study group to examine various proposals regarding the creation of reserve assets either through the IMF or otherwise." The study of the so-called adjustment problem, the problem of avoiding or removing major and persistent imbalances in international payments, was entrusted to Working Party 3 of the OECD.

The *Report of the Study Group on the Creation of Reserve Assets: Report to the Deputies of the Group of Ten* was published in August 1965. It became known as the report of the Ossola Committee, after Signor Rinaldo Ossola of the Bank of Italy, who had chaired the study group. The report described and analyzed "different means, other than new accruals of gold and reserve currency balances, of providing new or additional reserve assets to be available when the need is felt."

In the course of the Annual Meeting of the Fund in September 1965, held in Washington, the Group of Ten instructed their Deputies to "determine and report to Ministers what basis of agreement can be reached on improvements needed in the international monetary system, including arrangements for the future creation of reserve assets, as and when needed, so as to permit adequate provision for the reserve needs of the world economy."

In frequent meetings, and with the assistance of the staff of the IMF, the Group of Deputies, under the dynamic chairmanship of

Dr. Otmar Emminger of the German Federal Bank, prepared the requested report in July 1966. It was published, for release on August 25, 1966, with a *Communiqué of the Ministers and Governors of the Group of Ten.* On the title page, the Emminger study was described as a report "on improvements needed in the international monetary system, including arrangements for the future creation of reserve assets, as and when needed. . . ."

The longest chapter was on "Deliberate Reserve Creation," but one member — France — "refrained from participating in the discussion and drafting" of most of it; and there was no unanimity on any particular scheme. (Five schemes were described in the Annex of the Report.) But there was a majority view: "Most of us favor, as part of a contingency plan, the creation of a new reserve unit by the limited group" of countries having "particular responsibilities" for the functioning of new international monetary arrangements and for "the financial backing for any newly created reserve assets" (§98 and §99 of the Report).

The Ministerial Meeting of the Group of Ten, meeting in The Hague on July 25 and 26, 1966, considered the Report of the Deputies and also a report of Working Party 3 of the OECD "on possible improvements in the balance-of-payments process." The Ministers and Governors "expressed the hope" that the work on the problem of adjustment would be continued by the OECD group and — with one country (France) abstaining — instructed their Deputies "to continue their studies on a number of unresolved questions" regarding the problem of liquidity. They "recommended a series of joint meetings" with the Executive Directors of the Fund. There was full agreement "that, at some point in the future, existing types of reserves may have to be supplemented by the deliberate creation of additional reserve assets."

The Annual Meeting of the Fund in September 1966, held in Washington, approved the arrangement of joint meetings. Most of the Governors of the Fund had made strong pleas in favor of a plan that included all members of the IMF, not only a limited group of countries. Four joint meetings of the Executive Directors of the Fund and the Deputies of the Ten were held subsequently: in

November 1966 (in Washington), January 1967 (London), April 1967 (Washington), and June 1967 (Paris). The Group of Ten met several times between these dates.

In the early months of 1967, an understanding among the members of the European Economic Community (EEC) changed the tune of the discussions within the Group of Ten. The emphasis shifted from plans for the creation of new reserve assets to much less ambitious proposals for the extension of credit facilities. In the late spring of 1967 it looked as if the views of France, on the one side, and the United Kingdom and United States, on the other side, were irreconcilable.

Rather suddenly, the chances for an understanding improved. On July 18, 1967, largely as a result of the last of the joint meetings with the IMF Directors, the Deputies of the Ten were able to agree on most points of a draft "Outline." This was completed and approved by the Ministers and Governors of the Ten in London on August 26, and by the Executive Directors of the Fund on September 9, 1967.

A resolution adopting the agreed Outline was unanimously passed by the Board of Governors of the IMF on September 29, 1967, at the conclusion of their Annual Meeting, held in Rio de Janeiro. The provisions of the Outline had then to be translated into Legalese, a task which the staff and the Executive Directors were charged to complete by March 31, 1968. The new Articles of Agreement (reproduced here in Appendix D) will then have to be ratified by three-fifths of the governments of the member countries having among them four-fifths of the total voting power.

Several members of the Fund demanded that at the same time some of the original Articles of Agreement, as adopted on July 22, 1944 at Bretton Woods, New Hampshire, be altered in order to meet "operational requirements" and achieve greater consistency with the new arrangements. (The modifications are described in Appendix C.)

2.

Agreement Despite Disagreement

We have often seen how disagreements among scholars were resolved when ambiguous language was replaced by clear formulations not permitting different interpretations. The opposite is true in politics. Disagreements on political matters, national or international, can be resolved only if excessively clear language is avoided, so that each negotiating party can put its own interpretation on the provisions proposed and may claim victory in having its own point of view prevail in the final agreement.

The Compromise of Bretton Woods

This recipe for compromising antagonistic positions without compromising the antagonists had worked in the negotiations for the Bretton Woods agreements, nearly a quarter of a century ago. What the nations adopted at Bretton Woods was based on an outline agreed between the United Kingdom and the United States, an outline that permitted these countries to put opposite interpretations on rather fundamental issues.

At that time, however, the conflict and its resolution related, not to words and word meanings, but to theoretical concepts and preconceptions. The British had wanted a system quite unlike the gold standard; the Americans a system most similar to the gold standard. Since the approved document avoided any references to these terms or to points specifically alluding to the conceptions in question, it was possible for Lord [John Maynard] Keynes to report to the British Parliament that the arrangements established by the agreement would have no resemblance to the gold standard and would not impose on the member countries the intolerable restraints inherent in the workings of the gold standard. At the same time, Assistant Secretary Harry Dexter White and Secretary Fred M. Vinson of the Department of the Treasury were able to explain to the United States Congress that the new arrangements would work very much like the gold standard, with its historic contributions to stability and discipline.

The British interpretation rested on a definition of the gold standard as a system in which the supply of money is regulated essentially by the flows of gold and where foreign-exchange rates cannot be adjusted even when the balance of payments shows the economy to be in fundamental disequilibrium. The American interpretation was based on a definition of the gold standard as a system in which the dollar was "defined" as a specified quantity of gold, and where the exchange rates of most currencies were maintained at fixed parities. Thus, both of the two opposite positions, for the gold standard and against it, have supposedly prevailed.

The Compromise of Rio de Janeiro

In the negotiations leading to the Rio Agreement, the seemingly irreconcilable positions were the French and the British-American with regard to the future provision of "international liquidity."

In 1965 the French had made a proposal for the creation of a new reserve asset, the "Collective Reserve Unit" (CRU), to be distributed among the important ten countries in proportion to their gold stocks. When other nations announced that they would approve of schemes to create CRU's, provided these new reserve assets were allocated among countries in quite different proportions, the French discarded their plan. The French position in the concluding negotiations was one of strong opposition to the "creation of new reserve assets." It conceded only the possible "extension of credit" to monetary authorities; this extension to be made only when really necessary, perhaps through a newly established "credit facility" in the Fund. The American, or Anglo-American, position had firmly embraced the proposal for the creation and allocation of "reserve units," assets held by monetary authorities as owned reserves, without obligation to repay the loans by which an agency of the Fund would have created the transferable liquid claims against itself. In the American conception, the reserve units distributed by the Fund would constitute a sort of international money for reserve purposes and for transactions among national monetary authorities.

This conflict was resolved, almost miraculously, by extraordinarily efficient mediators applying the recipe of avoiding all the words which the nations had written on their banners and for which they were valiantly battling. The words "credit," "credit facility," "reserve asset," "reserve units," "borrowed reserves," "owned reserves," "loans," "repayments"— all of them were, with great circumspection, avoided in the Outline drafted. Words not burdened with a history of controversy, not associated with recognizable ideologies, and not widely used in monetary theories, words, therefore, with still neutral and not always fixed connotations were put in place of the old, battle-scarred and now banished words.

To be exact, the phrase "reserve assets" is allowed a single appearance in the first sentence of the Outline; however, it is used not for what is to be newly created but only in a safe reference to "existing reserve assets." The Outline is of a "facility"— mind you, not "credit facility," as some news analysts erroneously reported — a facility "intended to meet the need, as and when it arises, for a supplement to existing reserve assets." "Supplement" to existing reserve assets *may* mean new reserve assets — hear, hear, American interpreters. But it *need* not mean this, for it is equally possible for existing reserve assets to be supplemented, as a source of liquidity, by non-assets, for example, by some lines of credit — hear, hear, French interpreters.

Again, to be quite exact, the word "unit" appears once in the document, but not as a designation of the subject or object of the new drawing rights, but only in connection with the "maintenance of gold value" [Section VI (b)]. There it is stated that "The unit of value for expressing special drawing rights will be equal to 0.888671 grams of fine gold." (The initiated know that this is also the gold equivalent of the United States dollar; so it evidently seemed more expedient to the writers of the Outline to avoid a supererogatory reference to the dollar.)

The controversy during the negotiations had been essentially about two supposedly irreconcilable principles: credit facilities versus reserve allocations. The ingenious solution was to strike out "credit" and "reserve," leaving "facility" and "allocation" without modifying terms. A facility is established to allocate something. What? Special Drawing Rights — SDR's.

All Winners, No Losers

Of course, the mere omission of words that are dear to one group but offensive to another does not make a workable plan. Yet, what the Governors of the 107 nations approved at Rio is indeed a plan for supplementing existing reserve assets, and a very ingenious, novel, and workable plan at that. It consists in the deliberate creation and allocation of special drawing rights which the participating countries will be obliged to accept from one another and for which they will surrender convertible currencies to the country that makes the "drawing." Thus, countries will surely regard their holdings of these rights as reserves and will probably (for reasons I shall explain later) treat them as assets in the balance sheets of the monetary authority.

What the omission of the controversial words accomplished was acceptability, not only of the future special drawing rights, but also of the plan to create them. It enabled each of the representatives of the parties to the agreement to go home and tell their heads of government that they had won. As a matter of fact, the Governors in Rio did not wait for their return to their home countries: they announced their victories in the same official speeches in which they indicated their assent to the agreement.

In their statements during the discussions in Rio, in part presumably for home consumption, the speakers for the Anglo-Saxon countries and the speaker for France found it possible to give mutually contradictory interpretations of the agreed plan. The French minister had the satisfaction that the Outline called the new arrangement a *facility* and said nothing about the creation of reserve assets or units. The Anglo-Americans were reassured by the Outline's repeated references to *allocations* without any mention of credit, lending, borrowing, or repayment.

Even on the novelty and importance of the agreed arrangements they disagreed. In their Report of July 1966, the Deputies of the Group of Ten had admitted that a plan of this sort "represents a bold venture." In his statement praising the agreement on the Outline by the Ministers and Governors of the Ten, at their meeting in London on August 26, 1967, Secretary Henry H. Fowler of the United States Treasury exulted about "one of the great days in the history of financial cooperation." In the same vein, Britain's Chancellor of the Exchequer James Callaghan spoke of "a great moment in the history of international monetary cooperation" and was sure that this "meeting in Rio de Janeiro takes its place in history." Australia's Treasurer William McMahon, in Rio, praised the achievements of "this novel and radical system." The Brazilian Finance Minister, Professor Delfim Netto (an economist), said that we are "on the threshold of a new era in the management of international monetary matters." And the President of The Netherlands Bank, Professor Jelle Zijlstra (also an economist), found that "a very important step has been made on the road to a more rational international monetary system." Yet, France's Minister of Economic Affairs and Finance Michel Debré insisted that "the special drawing rights provision in no way constitutes a revolutionary step."

"These rights," Debré went on, "do not and cannot establish a new currency designed to replace gold. If such were the purport of the agreement, it is quite clear that France would not sign it. The plan provides for the possible extending of credit facilities." Contrast this with the statements from the other side: "No longer," said Callaghan, "will . . . the rate of growth of world reserves in total be dependent so largely on the rate of supply of new gold and the balance-of-payments positions of reserve centers." According to McMahon, the need was for "creating additional reserves for all countries," and the new system does in fact provide "for the creation of a new reserve asset which will be available unconditionally and automatically and will be permanent in character." And Secretary Fowler of the United States had this to say with regard to the purport of the agreement: "My country subscribes strongly to the view that the new facility is designed to assure a satisfactory rate of growth in global reserves."

The Germans had done much to mediate between the contradictory positions in the course of the negotiations. It was perhaps for this reason that Minister of Economics Kurt Schiller took pains to give aid and comfort to the French interpretation of the agreed provision of special drawing rights. He pronounced: "The new mechanism for the expansion of liquidity is based on the principles of credit and repayability. This is the right combination." But he added: "As in the national field, money is created by credit."

If there is genuine agreement on the actual arrangements, how is it possible that there is continuing disagreement on their interpretation? This question I must try to answer in a later section. I shall attempt to show that the differences are not "philosophic," as one mediator has remarked, but rather semantic and theoretic. However, before the semantic fog can be profitably dispelled and before some confused arguments of monetary theory can be cleared up, I must first examine the new system in both its essence and its details, then explore the background of the negotiations that led to its adoption and, finally, I shall set forth the implications of its eventual operation.

3.

The New System

The Spanish translation of special drawing rights is *derechos especiales de giro,* which expresses, much better than the English and French designations, the essential character of the scheme. The word "drawing" may suggest that less remains in the system after some of the rights have been exercised and certain amounts "drawn out." The word "giro," on the other hand, suggests transfer from one account to another, a gyration or circulation of amounts that, once created, remain in existence. A giro-right exercised by its holder merely passes on to another holder.

The Giro System
and the Allocation of Giro Balances

The new mechanism is, in fact, a payments system among central banks (monetary authorities) in which initial balances and later additional balances (probably in annual installments) are allocated to all participants in certain proportions — corresponding to their IMF quotas [III, 2 (ii)] — and from which no balances can be withdrawn — except when a participant withdraws altogether from the system or when the entire system is liquidated. (There is also a provision about cancellation of balances [IV], but this is not very likely ever to occur.) Thus, in principle, the sum total of balances (SDR's) on the current accounts of the participating countries, entered in the accounting records of a newly established Special Drawing Account, will grow over the years and will probably never decline. The use of its balance (SDR) by a participating country does not reduce the total of balances (SDR's) in the system, because the balance used by one accrues to another. Since transfers are permitted only among the closed group of participants, never to anyone outside the system, there can be no net outflow from the system.

The word "participant" is used throughout the Outline, evidently in order to distinguish it from "member." To be sure, only members of the Fund may become participants in the Special Drawing Account. But, while every participant has to be a member, not every member has to be a participant. To allow for this possibility, the separate designation of participant was provided.

The primary purpose of the scheme is, of course, to create balances in the participants' accounts in order to meet a need for a supplement to existing reserve assets, as and when it arises. The "as and when" as well as the "how much," that is, the times and amounts of allocations, will be determined — upon a recommendation of the Managing Director, concurred in by the Executive Directors — ultimately by the Board of Governors, voting with an 85 per cent majority [Section III, 5(a)]. (Thus, in effect, the members of the European Common Market, who now have a combined voting power of more than 16.4 per cent, will have a veto power if they vote as a bloc.) As a rule, amounts of allocations are to be determined in advance for "basic periods" of five years [III,2(i)]. Such long-run decisions have the advantage that hasty decisions under the impression of pressures of the moment are avoided; but exceptions are permitted by the Outline.

The "considerations" and "principles" to be used in decisions about times and amounts of allocations have not yet been formulated, but will be included in an introductory section to the Amendment [III, 1]. The Managing Director will make a "proposal for the first basic period" only after he has satisfied himself that there is "broad support among the participants to start the allocation" of the SDR's [III,3(c)]. This provision probably serves to avoid the embarrassment of a veto (that is, of an opposition of more than 15 per cent of the votes). As a further protection for unwilling participants, a country that has not voted for a particular allocation of SDR's need not receive any "under that decision," that is, it may "opt out" of further participation beyond a stipulated amount [III,6].[1]

Some critics have commented on the absence of any indication in the Outline of the probable order of magnitude of total allocations. In the discussions, annual allocations of between $1,000 million and $2,800 million had been mentioned. The decision to omit any references to the amount was partly motivated by the consideration that any amount that looks reasonable now may be unrealistically small by the time of the first allocation. Again, in all discussions, there was a strong sentiment in favor of determining the allocation of special drawing rights in the light of any possible additions to total reserves from other sources, especially gold and dollars. On the other hand, there was opposition to fixing annual increments to total reserves and letting the creation of SDR's be determined by the otherwise unfulfilled portion.[2] While changes in the gold and currency reserves will undoubtedly be taken into consideration when the size of SDR allocations is decided, the negotiators did not, at this time, want to adopt any formula.

The Use of SDR's

A participant may use its SDR's for transfers to another participant in order to acquire — for legitimate purposes mentioned below —"an equivalent amount of a currency convertible in fact" [V, 1(a)]. Ordinarily, this will be the currency of a third country; for example, if Denmark transfers SDR's to Italy, this will most likely be in ex-

---

[1] The "opting-out" provisions formulated on the basis of the Outline did not satisfy some of the countries. At a conference of the Ministers and central-bank Governors of the Group of Ten, held in Stockholm on March 29-30, 1968, on the new articles of agreement prepared by the Executive Directors of the Fund, changes were negotiated to give more protection to participants reluctant to accept additional SDR's. (Appendix D will show the final version submitted for ratification.)

[2] Under such a scheme, the Board would fix the total increment desired at, say, 4 per cent of total reserves, or $2,800 million, for the first year; it would then find that, for example, $100 million worth of gold had been added to the monetary gold stock and $400 million of dollar assets had been acquired by national monetary authorities; it would conclude that this had left a deficiency of $2,300 million to be made up by the allocation of SDR's. No such scheme has found favor with the majority.

change for United States dollars. In certain instances, however, for example, when the United States is involved in the transaction, the currency may be that of the participant *using* SDR's or that of the participant *receiving* SDR's. The first of these cases is provided for in the Outline, when it states that "a participant may use its special drawing rights to purchase balances of its currency held by another participant, with the agreement of the latter" [V,3(d)]. While such a repurchase of dollars by the United States with SDR's is not permitted "for the sole purpose of changing the composition of its reserves" [V,1 (c)], it may be resorted to in order to prevent a loss of gold through conversion of dollars held by other participants. The other possibility — that a participant receiving SDR's gives its own currency in exchange — is not mentioned in the Outline, but seems almost inevitable when the holdings of the participant that is drawn upon do not include sufficient amounts of foreign currency, as in the case of the United States. If the United States were not permitted to deliver dollars in exchange for SDR's, it would either be forced to carry larger amounts of foreign currencies or it would have to procure them on each occasion through a sale of gold.

In general, "a participant will be expected" to use its SDR's only for two legitimate purposes: "balance-of-payments needs" and "in the light of developments in its total reserves" [V, 1(c)]. The second of these clauses again chiefly reflects the special circumstances of the United States, which may lose gold even while its payments balance is not in deficit. (Since countries may convert dollar holdings into gold, it is perfectly appropriate to enable the United States to purchase such dollar holdings from them with its SDR's.) But the purposes of particular transfers "will not be subject to prior challenge," that is, the right to make transfers is unconditional within certain quantitative limits. However, if the Fund finds that a participant has failed to observe the "expectations" regarding the appropriate uses of its SDR's, the Fund "may direct drawings to such participant to the extent of such failure" [V,1(d)]. That is to say, if a participant has used, say, ten million dollars worth of its SDR's for inappropriate purposes (for example, in order to use the currency received for purchases of gold), the Fund may advise other participants to use the same amount of their SDR's for transfers to the misbehaving participant, forcing him thereby to surrender the currency improperly acquired.[3]

The selection of "the participants from which currencies should be acquired" by users of SDR's will follow certain rules and instructions of the Fund. Normally, countries will be chosen "that have a sufficiently strong balance of payments" or a "strong reserve position even though they have moderate balance-of-payments deficits" [V,3(a)]. A "primary criterion will be to seek to approach over time equality among the participants" in the ratios of SDR holdings, or of excess holdings, to total reserves, at least for countries with strong reserve positions [V,3(b)]. Finally, the choice of the country to be drawn upon and thus to receive SDR's may be determined by the desire to build up the SDR holdings of those that have previously drawn them down and are supposed to reconstitute them [V,3(c) and V,4].

To what extent these rules and criteria are consistent, or may call for further thought to reconcile inconsistencies in certain circumstances, will be examined later.

Quantitative Limits on Use and Acceptance

Quite apart from the periodic decisions concerning the allocation of additional SDR's in specific amounts expressed as percentages of quotas, there will be quantitative limits of the amounts a partici-

---

[3] An illustration may help one understand some of the provisions described in the two preceding paragraphs. Assume a country that prefers gold to dollar holdings has recently acquired large amounts of dollars. The United States, anticipating that these dollars may momentarily be presented for conversion into gold, can ask the country in question whether it would surrender its excess dollars in exchange for a transfer of SDR's. If the United States has a payments deficit at the time, the other country will surely not refuse this exchange. If the United States happened not to be in a deficit position, and if the other country were unwilling to surrender the dollars to the United States in exchange for SDR's (preferring to use them for getting gold), the Fund could resort to its prerogative of "directing" drawings. It could direct the drawings of deficit countries to the participant with the excessive holdings of dollars. If that country had in the meantime converted all its dollars into gold, it would have to sell the gold again in order to get the convertible currency (dollars) needed to honor the SDR's presented by the deficit countries.

pant is *able to use* and of the amounts a participant is *obliged to accept.*

Strictly speaking, no limits are provided on the use of SDR's, but in effect the obligation of users to reconstitute their positions up to certain minimum amounts will operate as limits on use. The rule for the first basic period of five years will be that "the average net use" of a participant's SDR's "shall not exceed 70 per cent of its average net cumulative allocation during this period" [V,4,(b)(i)].

In rough and ready terms this means that each participant is supposed to carry a minimum balance of 30 per cent of the allocations received. In more precise terms, however, a participant may carry lower balances for some years if the shortfall will be compensated by higher balances in later years; or *vice versa.* But what is high or low will depend on the cumulative allocations received. If a participant's balance in the first year was, on the average, 40 per cent of the first allocation, and the balance in the second year 25 per cent of the sum of the first and second allocations, and so forth, it will be quite a trick for a deficit country to "plan" for a balance of no less than 30 per cent over five years, especially if future allocations are still uncertain. The Outline wisely provides for a review of these rules before the end of the first period, though their amendment or abrogation requires an 85 per cent majority vote.

The limits on the obligation to accept are less complicated: no participant is obliged to hold more than three times its own cumulative allocations [V,2][4]. Thus, if a member country has, over the years, been allocated $100 million worth of SDR's, it must accept another $200 million worth of SDR's from member countries in weaker reserve positions; it may agree to take even more.

Since the Outline contains no terminology for a participant country's holdings of SDR's in excess of its cumulative allocations, I propose to call them "excess holdings." Borrowing from analogous Fund terminology, I propose to speak of "super-excess holdings"

---

[4] "A participant's obligation to provide currency will not extend beyond a point at which its holdings of special drawing rights in excess of the net cumulative amount of such rights allocated to it are equal to twice that amount. However, a participant may provide currency, or agree with the Fund to provide currency, in excess of this limit" [V,2].

when the reference is to holdings in excess of the upper limit to the participant's obligation to receive SDR's, that is, in excess of an amount three times the cumulative allocations.

It may be interesting to examine the numerical relationship between the two limits, the (implicit) limit to use SDR's and the (explicit) limit to the obligation to accept SDR's from other participants. This will be done here with reference to the rights and commitments of the United States under the provisions of the Outline. The calculation will be based on the present quota of the United States — 24.6 per cent as of June 1967 — and on the (arithmetically simple) assumption that an initial allocation of SDR's is made in a total amount of $1,000 million. Thus $246 million would go to the United States and $754 million to other countries (provided that all member countries participate in the system).

If the United States decides to apply its use limit not only to the average over five years but also to the first year, it must count on holding a minimum balance of 30 per cent of its allocation, or $74 million; if its balance of payments is in deficit, it would be able to use $172 million of the $246 million allocated. If the countries of the European Economic Community ("the Six," but in monetary affairs, because of the link between Belgium and Luxembourg, only "the Five") were all in payments surplus, they would be obliged to accept from other participants SDR's in an amount up to twice the allocations they had received. Their combined quota of 17.8 per cent of the total (as of June 30, 1967) would have made them recipients of $178 million in SDR's and would oblige them to accept another $356 million in SDR's. This would amply accommodate the maximum which the United States would be safe to use.

If, instead, all other countries, and not the United States, were in deficit — not a likely story in the near future — and observed the five-year use limit also for the first year, they could use a maximum of $528 million of the allocation of $754 million. If the United States had a surplus in its balance of payments, it would be obliged to accept from other participants SDR's in an amount up to twice the allocation it had received. Thus, with the allocation of $246 million, the obligation of the United States to accept SDR's from others would be $492 million (hence, not the entire $528 million which the others could use if they all were in deficit and every country wanted to keep 30 per cent of its allocation as a minimum balance). The maximum holding obligation of the United States would be three times its allocation, or $738 million of the total of $1,000 million allocated to all countries together.

A Hierarchy of Rules for Transfers

The reading of the rules which are to guide participants and the Special Drawing Account in their decisions about what I dare to call the pecking order, that is, decisions on which are the most eligible countries to be drawn upon, may be somewhat bewildering. These rules seem inconsistent, though some of the inconsistencies disappear upon closer examination. The following rules or guidelines can be found in the Outline:

1. Direct the drawing to countries with sufficiently strong payments positions and/or reserve positions. This is not always conclusive, since a country may have a satisfactory payments surplus but still a weak reserve position, and another country may run a moderate payments deficit but still have a strong reserve position [V,3(a)]. Moreover, the strength of the reserve position cannot be unambiguously measured: reserves may bear different relations to different relevant magnitudes (such as national income, value of imports, domestic money supply, liquid foreign liabilities).

2. Direct the drawing to countries with relatively low ratios of SDR holdings to total reserves [V,3(b)].

3. Direct the drawing to countries with relatively low ratios of excess holdings of SDR's to total reserves [V,3(b)].

4. Direct the drawing to countries with large holdings of reserve currencies (which may otherwise be converted into gold and which these countries are willing to exchange against SDR's) [V,3(d)].

5. Direct the drawing to countries which are expected to reconsti-

tute their holdings of SDR's after having them depleted to an undue extent or for inappropriate purposes [V,3(c) and V,4].

The inconsistencies can be reduced by the following considerations: (a) The second and third of these rules are possibly alternative proposals between which a choice may be made when the definitive provisions are formulated.[5] The differences between these alternative approaches to what may be called the "equality criterion" will be discussed presently. (b) The fourth rule is not a criterion for guidance by the Special Drawing Account but refers only to transactions which participants may make without guidance. (c) The fifth rule is placed in a different section of the Outline, namely, with the provisions for reconstitution.

The remaining inconsistencies can be explained as differences between day-to-day procedural rules and the long-run objectives expressed in the "equality criterion." The Outline, incidentally, alludes to still another principle, which we may call the "balance criterion." It is formulated as the "desirability of pursuing over time a balanced relationship between their [the participants'] holdings of special drawing rights and other reserves" [V,4,(b) (ii)]. This sentence is placed in the section on reconstitution and no techniques are mentioned by which the "desirability" of "balanced" composition of reserves might be implemented.

The equality criterion is called, in the Outline, the "primary criterion," but it is clearly only a long-run target. It is the approach over time to "equality among the participants . . . in the ratios of their holdings of special drawing rights, or such holdings in excess of net cumulative allocations thereof, to total reserves" [V,3 (b)]. The international comparisons of these ratios presuppose, of course, acceptance of consistent definitions and measurements of "total reserves."

For these comparisons one has to compute, for any point of time, the ratio of the total SDR's in existence to the total reserves of all participants taken together, and compare with that the ratio of each country's holdings of SDR's to its total reserves and, alterna-

---

[5] See Appendix D, not available to the author at the time of writing.

tively, the ratio of its excess holdings to its total reserves. It may prove difficult to agree on a consistent definition of "reserves"— think of the claims and liabilities arising from swap operations, of official holdings of foreign securities with maturities over more than twelve months, or in general of the difference between gross and net reserves. Under any definition, however, we shall find that the *comparative* excess holdings of participants — that is, holdings of SDR's above those that would satisfy the criterion of equality — are different from their *absolute* excess holdings, defined on the basis of cumulative allocations. This is so because the reserves held by the participating countries bear proportions to the total of reserves held by the entire group that are very different from their relative quotas in the Fund and, hence, from the relative allocations of SDR's. (See Table 1.)

Thus, even on the first day after the allocation of SDR's, before any transfers of SDR's have occurred, some countries (namely, those with low reserves relative to their quotas) will have comparative excess holdings of SDR's or, as I propose to call them, "supra-equi-proportional" holdings. Conversely, countries with small quotas relative to reserves will have been allocated relatively small amounts of SDR's and will have to accept, in the course of time and to the extent that they have payments surpluses, large amounts of SDR's from other participants before their balances will reach amounts that would represent equiproportional holdings.

For example, in June 1967, the countries of the European Economic Community had a combined quota of 17.9 per cent of the total quota in the Fund, but their combined reserves were 36.1 per cent of the total reserves held by the members. The differences between shares in total quota and shares in total reserves are relatively unimportant as far as the two reserve-currency countries are concerned, provided the calculations are based on gross reserves. Thus, the United Kingdom had 11.6 per cent of all quotas and 4.2 per cent of reserves, and the United States had 24.6 per cent of all quotas and 21.1 per cent of reserves. The difference is quite small for the other three members of the Group of Ten. Sweden, Canada, and Japan together had 8 per cent of all quotas and 8.4 per cent

Table 1

QUOTAS AND GROSS RESERVES OF MEMBERS, AS OF
JUNE 30, 1967
(in dollars and percentages)

COUNTRY OR GROUP OF COUNTRIES	QUOTA IN IMF		GROSS RESERVES INCLUDING IMF RESERVE POSITIONS	
	IN MILLIONS OF DOLLARS	IN % OF TOTAL	IN MILLIONS OF DOLLARS	IN % OF TOTAL
Belgium (including Luxembourg)	438	2.1	2,457	3.6
France	985	4.6	6,688	9.9
Germany	1,200	5.7	7,794	11.5
Italy	625	2.9	4,965	7.3
Netherlands	520	2.4	2,471	3.6
Subtotal: The Five	3,768	17.9	24,375	36.1
Sweden	225	1.0	1,007	1.4
Canada	740	3.5	2,630	3.9
Japan	725	3.5	2,099	3.1
Subtotal: The Eight	5,458	26.0	30,111	44.7
United Kingdom	2,440	11.6	2,834	4.2
United States	5,160	24.6	14,270	21.1
Subtotal: The Ten	13,058	62.2	47,215	70.1
Other Europe (excluding Switzerland)	1,391	6.6	5,938	8.8
Australia	500	2.3	1,542	2.2
New Zealand	157	.7	122	.1
South Africa	200	.9	639	.9
Latin America	1,866	8.8	3,415	5.0
Middle East	661	3.2	2,990	4.4
Other Asia	2,247	10.7	3,898	5.7
Other Africa	891	4.2	1,576	2.3
Subtotal: The Other 96	7,913	37.8	20,120	29.8
Total: All 106	20,971	100.0	67,335	100.0

Note: Details may not add to totals due to rounding.

SOURCE: International Monetary Fund, *International Financial Statistics*.

of reserves. The other 96 member countries, however, had larger shares in total quotas than in total reserves: their combined quota was 37.8 per cent of all quotas, and their combined reserves 29.8 per cent of the total reserves held by all members.

The approach to equality in the ratio of SDR holdings to reserves would, therefore, make the Five the favorite net recipients of SDR's, and the 96 countries the most eligible net users. Latin America, "other Asian," and "other African" countries seem to have the strongest claims on the Five, if the figures are correct and if the approach to equiproportional holdings of SDR's is to be speedy. Some of the statistic of quotas may, however, call for considerable corrections with regard to countries that have paid only small parts of their subscriptions.[6] Moreover, the Five, especially France, Germany, and Italy, may find their quotas unduly low in the light of past developments and future possibilities, and they may call for adjustments at the next round of quota revisions. Still, with all possible corrections and adjustments, it remains true that, on the first day after the allocation of SDR's, there will be no country with excess holdings but many countries with supra-equiproportional holdings of SDR's. And, even after some time, perhaps years, a few countries with substantial excess holdings may still have less than their equiproportional share of SDR's.

To mention these complications of the "primary criterion" for choosing participants on which drawings should be made is not to disparage it. On the contrary, since allocations of SDR's will be in proportion to quotas, rather than in proportion to total reserves, the gradual changes in the distribution of SDR holdings through drawings in conformance with the equality criterion are quite appropriate. They will be in the "right" direction from countries with weaker to countries with stronger reserve positions.

Similar statements could be made regarding the "balance criterion" mentioned among the provisions for reconstitution: "Participants will pay due regard to the desirability of pursuing over time a balanced relationship between their holdings of special drawing rights

---

[6]The case of Nationalist China (Taiwan) stands out in this respect.

and other reserves" [V,4(b)(ii)]. No rules concerning techniques of attaining this "principle" are contained in the Outline. Those involved in the negotiations know how much sweat — though no tears and no blood — had gone into the effort of formulating (and deformulating) workable rules for the harmonization of the "reserve mix" among the participating countries. The reference to the "desirability" of balance in reserve holdings may turn out to be only a reminder of valiant efforts that have come to naught.

A Glossary of Terms to Fit the Rules

The foregoing considerations suggest the need for a terminology that allows us to handle the various concepts with greater economy of words. Moreover, the availability of terms that fit the rules may aid the operators, the directors, the analysts, and the lawyers to achieve a better understanding of the ideas involved. In proposing suitable terms, I am not so immodest as to hope that the insiders will readily adopt them; they may find words that sound better or they may be too proud to accept an outsider's coinage. But I certainly cannot wait for their linguistic product; the terms are needed right now for the present exposition. Here, then, is my glossary referring to the holdings of SDR's by a participating country:

SDR HOLDINGS . . . . current balance of SDR's held by a participant; it will be the result of cumulative allocations received, *minus* amounts used, *plus* amounts received in transfers, *plus* interest credited, *minus* the share in interest cost assessed.

SDR EXCESS HOLDINGS . . . . the participant's SDR holdings in excess of cumulative allocations received.

SDR SUPER-EXCESS HOLDINGS . . the participant's SDR holdings in excess of three times the cumulative allocations received.

EQUIPROPORTIONAL
SDR HOLDINGS . . . . the participant's hypothetical SDR holdings in an amount that bears to the participant's total reserves the same ratio that total SDR's in existence bear to the total reserves of all participants taken together.

EQUIPROPORTIONAL
SDR EXCESS HOLDINGS . . . . . the participant's hypothetical SDR excess holdings in an amount that bears to the participant's total reserves the same ratio that total positive excess holdings of SDR's bear to the total reserves of all participants, both excess holders and net users, taken together.

SUPRA-EQUIPROPORTIONAL
SDR HOLDINGS . . . . the participant's actual SDR holdings in excess of the participant's equiproportional SDR holdings.

SUPRA-EQUIPROPORTIONAL
SDR EXCESS HOLDINGS . . . . . the participant's actual SDR excess holdings over and above the participant's equiproportional excess holdings.

The operators of the Special Drawing Account may want to have before them an up-to-date tabulation of the standing of all participants with regard to the magnitudes just defined. In addition, they should have data on the participants' reserve positions — size as well as composition — and also the changes in these positions that have occurred (perhaps annual changes over the last five years and monthly changes over the last 18 months).

Keeping these tabulations up to date will call for continuing recomputation, because the total reserves of the group may be affected by transactions among participants. This is most likely to be the case if SDR's are used by or vis-à-vis a reserve-currency country, which could affect the amounts of dollars (or pounds) held in official reserves, or if drawings on or repurchases from the General Account of the Fund are made that affect the total size of gold-tranche positions.[7]

Thus, several types of international transactions will change not only the reserve positions and SDR holdings of participants but also the size and composition of the reserves of all participants taken together. This will alter several numbers in the calculation of equiproportional and supra-equiproportional SDR holdings.

One of the tabulations that may prove useful to the operators and analysts of the Special Drawing Account is as follows:

MODEL OF A CONVENIENT TABULATION

OF PARTICIPANTS' CURRENT SDR POSITIONS

	(1)	(2)	(3)	(4)	(5)
Participating Country	SDR Holdings	Cumulative SDR Allocations	Positive SDR Excess Holdings $(1) - (2)$	Positive SDR Super-Excess Holdings $(1) - [3 \times (2)]$	Total gross reserves incl. IMF reserve position

(6)	(7)	(8)	(9)
Equiproportional SDR Holdings $\dfrac{\Sigma(1)}{\Sigma(5)} \times (5)$	Equiproportional SDR Excess Holdings $\dfrac{\Sigma(3)}{\Sigma(5)} \times (5)$	Supra-equiproportional SDR Holdings $(1) - (6)$	Supra-equiproportional SDR Excess Holdings $(3) - (7)$

[7] See footnote on page 28.

Collaboration, Compulsion, and Incentives

Since the success of the whole scheme depends on the acceptability of the SDR's on the part of the monetary authorities of the participating countries, the Outline provides for a plea for collaboration [VIII,1], sanctions for nonfulfillment of obligations [VIII,2], and incentives for holders of SDR's in the form of interest payments [VI(a)] and gold-value guarantees [VI(b)].

The sanction for failure to fulfill the obligation to honor SDR's (by providing currency in exchange) consists in the suspension of the delinquent country's right to use its own SDR's. (If that country has drawn down its SDR's to or below the minimum balance, suspension of its further SDR's may not look like an effective deterrent, except for the expectation of future allocations. But the danger that there will be many cases of nonfulfillment is probably slight.) For other violations, the sanction is suspension of the right to use such SDR's as are acquired after the verdict. Suspension of a participating country's rights does not affect its obligations.

Interest will be paid on all balances, at a "moderate rate," in the form of additions to the SDR balances. That is, interest will be credited to the current accounts. The cost will be assessed to all participants in proportion to the cumulative allocations. A good accountant contemplating the appropriate procedures will visualize a balance sheet of the Special Drawing Account having on the assets side the Allocation Accounts of all participants and on the liabilities side the Current Accounts of all participants. The Current Accounts will show the balances on which interest has to be credited, the Allocation Accounts will show the proportions in which the cost of

---

(footnote referred to on page 27)

[7] To illustrate the variability of reserve-currency holdings, assume that the United States uses SDR's to repurchase dollars held by a participant that agrees to this exchange. The total of SDR's is unchanged, but the total of dollar reserves is reduced.

To illustrate the variability of gold-tranche positions in the Fund, assume that a member with a gold-tranche position makes a drawing on the General Account of the Fund to obtain the currency of a country that has used much of its credit tranche. As a result, the total gold-tranche positions are reduced, because the partial restoration of credit-tranche positions does not count in reserve statistics.

total interest payments will have to be shared. Both the credits and the debits arising from this operation will be entered on the Current Accounts; as a result, the credit balances of "excess holders" of SDR's will be increased, those of "net users" of SDR's will be reduced, and the total credit balances will remain unchanged.

This mental picture of an accounting procedure should not confuse us regarding an important point: the Allocation Accounts on the assets side of the balance sheet do not represent assets of the Fund, and the Current Accounts on the liabilities side do not represent liabilities of the Fund. The Special Drawing Account of the Fund is merely an agent and bookkeeper for the participating countries. It owns nothing and owes nothing.

Those who wonder how high or how low a "moderate" rate of interest may actually be will appreciate a clue. In the discussions a rate of 1.5 per cent per annum has been mentioned as adequate. This is less than the yield on certain dollar reserve assets, but surely a great deal more than the zero earnings on gold. Several central-bank managers have indicated that they would consider SDR holdings as highly attractive assets in their monetary reserves.

There is, finally, the gold-value guarantee. This provision of the agreed Outline calls for a more extended discussion, because what may be greater "security" for one party in a transaction is usually greater "risk" for another party.

The Gold-Value Guarantee

"The unit of value for expressing special drawing rights will be equal to 0.888671 grams of fine gold. The rights and obligations of participants and of the Special Drawing Account will be subject to an absolute maintenance of gold value or to provisions similar to Article IV, Section 8, of the Fund's Articles" [VI,(b)].

The cited Section of the original Fund Agreement describes the obligations of a member country in the event that the par value of its currency is reduced or increased; Subsection (d) states that the same provisions "shall apply to a uniform proportionate change in the par value of the currencies of all members, unless at the time when such a change is proposed the Fund decides otherwise." Evidently it is this potential exception in the case of a uniform proportionate change in the gold parities which in the Outline is referred to as the alternative to an "absolute maintenance of gold value." Some representatives of the Group of Ten claim, however, that this alternative was expressly excluded in one of their agreed pronouncements and would, therefore, not be acceptable to them. Absolute maintenance of the agreed gold value of the SDR's implies that even in the case of a universal increase (decrease) in the price of gold, which would leave all foreign-exchange rates unchanged, one "unit" of SDR would command an increased (reduced) amount of currencies.

While most central bankers regard absolute gold-value maintenance of a reserve asset as a diminution of the risk of holding it and as a condition for confidence in it, some economists see serious risks for countries using or accumulating SDR's with gold-value clauses. In the case of a sharp increase in the price of gold (in terms of national currencies), countries that have used large portions of their SDR's might have to reconstitute them, sooner or later, at prices much higher in terms of exports and imports than prevailed at the time they drew down their balances. In the case of a reduction of the price of gold, countries that have accumulated large amounts of SDR's might suffer a loss of real purchasing power. The question is whether those risks are serious.

Before March 1968, one would probe this question on the basis of an analysis of the forces that might affect supply and demand in the gold market in years to come. For it was generally assumed that the value of gold was measured by the price of gold in the London market. The London price was pegged by interventions of the Bank of England, acting for a group of the most powerful gold-holding nations of the world. Gold was purchased for monetary authorities whenever supply exceeded private demand; and sales out of monetary stocks were made whenever private supply fell short of private demand. Until 1965, purchases for monetary authorities kept the market price of gold from falling below $35 an ounce; after that year their sales kept the price from rising. What had happened to private supply and demand?

There had been a large increase in gold production, mainly because of the discovery of rich gold fields in South Africa.[8] But there had also been a large increase in private demand for gold, partly for industrial use, for jewelry, and for accumulations by traditional hoarders in the Middle East, India, and Southeast Asia. The increase in private demand was expected to go on forever, while the increase in output was leveling off. Propaganda by gold-mining interests helped to impress on many people, laymen as well as financial experts, the strong belief that an increase in the price of gold was inevitable. In consequence, although new production was still far in excess of purchases by processors and traditional hoarders, the demand by speculators grew increasingly buoyant until the interventions in the London market became too expensive for the United States as the chief, or almost sole, supplier of monetary gold to the market. A gold pool comprising most or all of the monetary gold of the free world could have fed virtually any potential private demand for many years to come, with no difficulty at all. Indeed, if it were not for speculative purchases, the market price would for several years need the support of purchases by monetary authorities; otherwise it would fall below $35 an ounce.

Reflections such as these became moot for the question of gold-value guarantees when, on March 17, 1968, official interventions in the London gold market were stopped by the seven active members of the gold pool. They agreed that "officially held gold should be used only to effect transfers among monetary authorities," that they would no longer "supply gold to the London gold market or any other gold market," and "that henceforth they will not sell gold to monetary authorities to replace gold sold in private markets." Moreover, "as the existing stock of monetary gold is sufficient in view of the prospective establishment of the facility for special drawing

---

[8] Gold production in South Africa had increased from $428 million in 1945 to $618 million in 1958 and to $1,081 million in 1966. Laymen often fail to comprehend the implied reduction in production cost: if at an unchanged selling price it becomes profitable to increase output, this is as a rule indicative of lower cost of production, not for individual firms but for the industry as a whole.

rights, they no longer feel it necessary to buy gold from the market."[9]

These decisions amount to a declaration of independence of the official gold price from the market price determined by supply and demand. Since the International Monetary Fund gave its blessing to this arrangement, it seems now established that "par values" of currencies expressed in terms of gold are not affected by variations in the market price of gold. This settles the question of whether the gold-value guarantee presents a danger to holder or users of SDR's. The guarantee retains its meaning for cases in which the par value of exchange of a currency is changed vis-à-vis other currencies and the official price of gold; but whether the price of gold in the market will fall to $25 or rise to $50 will not be relevant.

A Few Sentences Between the Lines

A few — astonishingly few — passages of the Outline seem obscure. The drafting committee must surely have had some special possibilities in mind, but did not tell what they were. I shall briefly touch on two such provisions.[10]

"The General Account will be authorized to hold and use special drawing rights" [II,2]. But how will it acquire them? Certainly not as a part of normal allocations, since these are only to participating countries in proportion to their quotas. Thus, the General Account could receive SDR's only from participants. Perhaps countries that have purchased foreign currencies from the General Account may repurchase their own currencies (that is, make their repayments) with SDR's; perhaps they may exchange SDR's for gold held by the General Account (if the General Counsel holds this to be permissible); perhaps they may pay Fund charges with their SDR's; or perhaps they may use SDR's in lieu of gold to pay for the gold

---

[9] The decision of the seven members of the gold pool puts into practice one of the proposals advanced by L. Albert Hahn in 1963. He recommended that central banks stop selling gold to "hoarders and speculators," stop also buying from them, and sell only to other central banks. L. Albert Hahn, "Anachronism of the Gold Price Controversy," *The Commercial and Financial Chronicle,* March 7, 1963. See also Fritz Machlup, *Plans for Reform of the International Monetary System,* (Princeton: International Finance Section, revised edition, 1964), pp. 70-71.

[10] Article XXV, Section 7 (see Appendix D), now throws light on this matter.

portion of their subscription of future increases in quotas. All these are mere hunches in an attempt to puzzle out what may have been intended by this provision.

Incidentally, the provisions limiting the uses of SDR's do not fit the General Account. This one holder is in several respects quite unlike all other holders of SDR's.

"A participant [using SDR's] may obtain the currencies . . . either directly from another participant or through the Special Drawing Account" [V,1(b)]. The preposition "through" evidently means "with the help or intermediation of." (After all, the Special Drawing Account does not hold currencies and, hence, cannot deliver currencies.) One wonders why the reference is necessary; it is clear from other provisions [e.g., V,3 and 4] that the Fund will issue "rules and instructions" and "rules and regulations" for the "selection of participants to be drawn upon" and for "directing drawings" in accordance with stated principles. The sense of the provision is probably to emphasize that a drawing participant need *not* ask for guidance from the Special Drawing Account, but may select the other party without direction. But this is a rather trivial matter, worrying only those who like to make sense of every word and every clause they read.

The Sense of the Whole Scheme

The plan as a whole makes eminently good sense. The more I study it the better I like it.[11]

The scheme is different from any of the many plans that had been proposed over the years of discussion. The chief difference is that it does not provide either credits from or claims against an international agency. Almost all previous plans, official or academic, for the creation of reserves had focused on a "central debtor" whose liabilities were to be the reserve assets of national monetary authori-

---

[11]My first, hasty judgment, expressed in an interview in August 1967, was too skeptical; it was based on early and misleading reports in newspapers about the creation of a "credit facility" with rigid "repayment obligations." The very recipe which allowed the reconciliation of conflicting positions had succeeded also in confusing the reporters — which, of course, is not very difficult in any case. Let me, then, retract my skeptical judgment expressed in the interview and substitute for it an expression of strong approval.

ties. This was true of the proposals for an international central bank; the proposals for an extended IMF; the proposals for collective or composite reserve units issued by an agency (of the Fund or separate) against deposits of national currencies; and the proposals of an agency acquiring securities issued to raise long-term capital for the finance of investments in developing countries. In the scheme now adopted there are no liabilities of the issuing agency: the Special Drawing Account is a record keeper of the current accounts of the participants, accounts that will be endowed with (initially and subsequently) allocated "credit balances" which will be acceptable to other participants just as national money is acceptable to members of a national community.

The liquidation of the fiction of the central debtor of money in circulation is a genuine breakthrough in monetary thinking. In the nation, no recipient, holder, or spender of money ever thinks of the existence of a legal debtor who issued the money and continues to "owe" something to the holder. The only thing in the mind of the recipient and holder of money is its transferability to and acceptability by others. The holder of money does not expect to "collect" from the issuing agency, but only to pass on the money to those who have something to sell. The holder of special drawing rights, likewise, will not collect from or draw on the Fund or its Special Drawing Account. Instead, the participating country will pass its SDR's on to other participants in payment for convertible currencies. In other words, the SDR's are international money accepted by the participating monetary authorities in payment for various convertible national currencies. Since only the acceptability of SDR's has to be secured, and is in fact secured by the obligations undertaken by the participants, there is no need for any obligation or liability to be assumed by the agency that issues or allocates them.

Debt-Money and Nondebt-Money

Within a nation, practically all money and near-money is somebody's debt. Bank notes are debts of the central bank; currency notes are debts of the national treasury; check deposits and time deposits in commercial banks are debts of these banks. Coins are an exception, but they are an insignificant part of the money supply.

The debt character of money has confused economists and lawyers for centuries: the fact that the recipient and holder of money has, on the one hand, taken over a legal claim against the issuer of the money and, on the other hand, acquired an economic claim against the rest of the community to be honored, when he so desires, in goods, services, or other titles to wealth, has been the source of perennial bafflement and endless twattle. The "loan" to the legal debtor and the "loan" to the community implied in the exchange of present for future goods or services have rarely been separated with sufficient clarity in the students' thinking.

In international transactions among monetary authorities, directly or indirectly, the acceptance and holding of convertible currencies and IMF reserve positions (of the "old" type) is also the acceptance of claims against other national and international authorities. At the same time, it is an act of conscious or unconscious "lending" to the world community by way of a surrender of present goods, services, or titles to wealth in exchange for a claim to the resources of other countries in an indefinite future. Only the acquisition of gold is free of the implication of lending in the legal sense and limited to that of lending in the economic sense. Gold is nobody's debt in the legal sense; it is, however, a claim to the world's resources as long as other nations (or at least one) are (is) willing to accept it in exchange for their (its) currencies and, indirectly therefore, for their (its) products, services, or other titles to wealth.

This character of gold, of being a claim to resources without being anybody's legal liability, is now being imparted to the deliberately created special drawing rights. Gold and SDR's will share the feature of being internationally acceptable in exchange for national currency without being a legal debt of any one nation, institution, or organization. There are, of course, some differences, chiefly technological and sociological. A technological difference lies in the fact that gold is heavy stuff in the vaults of a national or international institution (though it is more often only a piece of paper certifying title to the yellow metal stored in the cellars of the Federal Reserve

Bank of New York),[12] whereas SDR's will, with regard to technology, be nothing but entries in the books kept by the Special Drawing Account of the Fund. A sociological difference lies in the fact that the acceptability of gold derives from historical practices anchored in the laws of the lands as well as in myths of long standing, whereas the acceptability of SDR's will derive from a novel international agreement hammered out in sophisticated negotiations and ultimately ratified by the legislatures of the countries concerned.

The similarities in the functions of gold and SDR's as reserve assets of monetary authorities have prompted some people to give the latter the nickname "paper gold." I doubt that such a designation can help people in comprehending the issues involved. After all, gold certificates printed on paper have existed for hundreds of years; they could with much better reason be given the designation "paper gold." I do not know whether this expression was meant to dignify or to disparage the new reserve asset, but in fact it does neither. If it is meant merely to remind people that SDR's, like gold, will be official reserve assets; that SDR's, like gold, will be "nondebt money" among monetary authorities; that SDR's were invented to supplement gold in the monetary reserves of the nations; and that SDR's may over the years assume very significant proportions, not unlike gold, in the world's total reserves; then one may resign oneself to the popularity of the journalistic references to "paper gold."

The Order of Magnitude

On June 30, 1967, the composition of official monetary reserves of noncommunist countries was as follows:

Gold	$40.5 billion, or	57.1 per cent
United States dollars	16.3 billion, or	22.9 per cent
United Kingdom pounds	6.4 billion, or	9.0 per cent
Other currencies	1.9 billion, or	2.7 per cent
IMF reserve positions	5.9 billion, or	8.3 per cent
Together	71.0 billion, or	100 per cent

---

[12]Gold owned by foreign countries is in the vaults of the Federal Reserve Bank of New York, whereas gold owned by the United States Treasury is at Fort Knox.

Assuming that these figures will not have changed very much by 1969, but that there will have been an allocation of two billion dollars in SDR's, one cannot say that anything of great numerical significance will have been added. SDR's would be less than 3 per cent of total reserves, and 5 per cent of monetary gold reserves.

Let us now try to look farther ahead, perhaps to 1979. Over these ten years, the average annual creation of SDR's may be three, four, or five billion dollars, so that a total of thirty, forty, or fifty billion dollars would be created. If monetary gold stocks will not have increased, and may even have declined (because of a private excess demand for gold at an unchanged price of gold), the amount of SDR's in official reserves may well have overtaken the amount of gold. If the present disinclination to letting reserve currencies grow significantly in the official holdings of monetary authorities continues, foreign exchange will have receded to third place in the monetary reserves of the nations. (If the authorities are intelligent, foreign exchange may even be replaced entirely by IMF reserve positions.)

This speculation about the future must not be taken for a prediction. One cannot know what will happen, for there are, no doubt, other possibilities. For example, gold production may become more plentiful either because of technological improvements (including alchemy) or because the majority of the United States Congress goes mad and increases the price of gold, or private gold hoarders get discouraged and, tired of losing 10 per cent a year in carrying charges, disgorge several billion dollars worth of gold out of their strong boxes, cellars, and holes in the ground. Or, several monetary authorities, especially of developing countries, may prefer to accumulate United States dollars as a monetary reserve with higher yield. Or, monetary authorities may eventually learn that more flexible foreign-exchange rates would reduce the amounts of reserves they need for financing payments deficits. Any of these developments would probably induce the Governors of the Fund to go slow in creating SDR's. So, let us bear in mind that the above ten-year projection of SDR allocations was based on the presupposition that monetary authorities would continue to desire gradual growth of their reserves and would neither be able to accumulate gold nor be prepared to accumulate dollars in their official holdings.

Those who find this presupposition reasonable will not be surprised if SDR's, the new reserve asset, over the years become the most important part of monetary reserves.

Why SDR'S Will Be Assets

Several skeptic observers have raised doubts concerning the preparedness of central banks or other monetary authorities to treat the SDR's as reserve assets. In reply, at least two Governors during the Rio discussions declared that their countries would not hesitate to regard SDR's as full-fledged monetary reserve. Secretary Fowler said this: "While each country will make its own decision, it is expected that these special drawing rights will be treated as first-line reserves. The United States intends to do so." Chancellor Callaghan said this: "I should like to make it clear that the United Kingdom intends to include the new drawing rights, when they are created, in their front-line reserves. We hope that other countries will do likewise. When the new drawing rights are treated in this way, it will be manifest that they are a supplement to existing reserve assets."

These declarations on behalf of two governments may possibly increase, rather than alleviate, any doubts about the intentions of governments that are less enthusiastic about the new plan and less emphatic about its "purport." I submit, however, that there is little reason for doubt, at least with regard to the treatment of excess holdings of SDR's by central banks, no matter whether their managers are or are not sympathetic to the whole scheme.

The point is that monetary authorities undertake the obligation to receive from other participants transfers of SDR's in exchange for convertible currency. Holdings of foreign currencies are, by any accounting principles, assets on the books of the holder. If a central bank surrenders some of its foreign-currency reserves against the SDR's transferred to its account (in the books of the Special Drawing Account), it cannot help showing in its balance sheet the reduction of one asset item and the increase of another. The only alternative would be to treat the surrender of foreign exchange as a charge against profit and capital — not a very likely solution to the accounting problem.

This accounting argument is cogent only with regard to SDR's received in excess of the direct allocations from the Special Drawing Account. But since SDR's are perfectly substitutable and cannot be distinguished as to origin or usability, it would be rather silly for accountants to treat SDR's received through allocation differently from SDR's received through transfer. They are indistinguishable on the balance sheet. There will be a difference, of course, regarding the offsetting entry for SDR's obtained through allocation. The offset could conceivably be a credit to capital, due to a donation received; but this would be poor practice in view of contingent obligations in the case of withdrawal or liquidation. Hence, the most appropriate accounting practice would be to enter, on the liabilities side of the balance sheet of the central bank (or other type of monetary authority), a dormant item, namely, the contingent liability arising from the allocations received from the Special Drawing Account of the Fund.

Such a dormant liability in the balance sheet would have the additional advantage of permitting a quick calculation of net use or excess holdings of SDR's. If the SDR holdings shown on the assets side are smaller than the dormant liability on the other side, the difference indicates the net use made up to the date of the balance sheet. An excess of SDR holdings over the dormant liability indicates excess holdings. Only a very obstreperous central-bank manager would resist this simple treatment of SDR's in the accounting records of his institution.

Finding a Name for the Creature

Let us remember the strange fact that the new creature called "special drawing rights" has not yet been given a name for the unit in which the amounts of these rights can be expressed. The Outline provides only that "the unit value for expressing special drawing rights will be equal to 0.888671 grams of fine gold." This fixes the gold equivalent of the unit, but it does not give it a name.

Perhaps one will name it SDR-Unit or Fund-Unit, but the fact is that the omission of any such designation from the Outline suggests that the parents of the new creature have not agreed on a proper name.

Could one be contented with calling them SDR's? This would be rather odd. The abbreviation SDR (or, in French, DTS for droits de tirage speciaux) will hardly be usable both as the description of the *ability* to draw and as the designation for the *object* drawn or for its *quantity*. Drawing rights must be rights to draw certain amounts of something and, since the objects to be drawn are convertible currencies and there exists a large variety of such currencies, it may prove unavoidable to find a name for the unit. Since participants will be allocated different amounts on their current SDR accounts, and since they will transfer various amounts to the accounts of other participants (in exchange for currencies in amounts calculated by certain rates of exchange) the amounts on the accounts must be expressible in numbers of *something*.

The Fund quotas are expressed in United States dollars. Should the SDR's likewise be denominated in United States dollars? I suspect that some governments of the participating countries would not like it; perhaps they have already said so, with the result that the word "dollar" does not appear in the document. But there are much stronger reasons against using the United States dollar as the denomination of the SDR's: the gold-value maintenance of SDR's implies that the dollar equivalent of an SDR unit would be changed if the gold-par of exchange of the United States dollar were to be changed. For example, a doubling of the dollar price of gold would mean that one unit of SDR's would be the equivalent of two United States dollars.

There is no intention on the part of the United States government to change the gold-par of exchange of the United States dollar; nor is there likely to be any good reason for such a change in the indefinite future. Still, it would be wrong to fix and guarantee the gold equivalent of the SDR unit and, nevertheless, express it in United States dollars, the gold equivalent of which is under the control of the United States Congress.

Perhaps the aversion to the word "unit" is an afterthought of the quarrels about "Collective Reserve" Units or "Reserve" Units. If these adjectives are gone, the word unit (IMF Unit, Fund Unit) may become acceptable. The lawyers and accountants will soon recognize that there *are* units; they have got to be given a name, even if it is only the generic name ("units") to be used as a proper name.

The Crucial 85 Per Cent Vote

The agreement that a voting majority of 85 per cent is needed for a decision on the timing, amount, and rate of allocation of SDR's, has raised some misgivings about the scheme actually coming to life. If France persists in her present attitude and can induce her partners in the European Economic Community to vote with her, the required voting majority will not materialize and the creation of SDR's will be postponed — and the entire plan will be kept in abeyance. How serious is the danger of this kind of procrastination?

Although it may be wishful thinking, I think that the present French attitude regarding deliberate creation of monetary reserves will either not continue or not prevail over that of her partners in EEC. Why not? For the simple reason that, if total reserves will have failed to increase, and perhaps will have declined, for one or two years, every intelligent observer and analyst will see that artificial respiration is required for the sake of world trade and production. A policy of "too little and too late" would lead to strong pressures by practically all member countries of the Fund and it is unlikely that the Five, or even France herself, would want to become isolated as deliberate perpetrators of sabotage against world prosperity.

In saying this, I have anticipated the conclusions of an inquiry into the purposes of creating international liquidity. This will be my next task.

4.

Background and Implications of the New System

Having examined the main features of the new system, I shall now turn to the elucidation of some of its implications that may prove important. There has been some confusion about the intended purposes of the creation of international liquidity as well as about possible though not intended consequences. Among the questions to be dealt with, I shall assess the liberalizing, the inflationary, and the resource-transferring influences that may make themselves felt and shall examine what comparative benefits, if any, may be derived from the operation of the system for less-developed countries, for chronic-deficit countries, and for reserve-currency countries. These reflections will incidentally make evident what should have been obvious from the outset, that the new system of securing an adequate growth of reserves is not designed to solve other international financial and monetary problems of equal, if not greater, importance.

The Purposes of Creating International Liquidity

The debate on the adequacy or inadequacy of international liquidity has been going on for years, but it does not seem that the issues have become clear to the participants any more than to the wider public. There is official disagreement on whether monetary reserves have for years been insufficient, are becoming insufficient now, or may become insufficient sometime in the future. Yet, how can there be agreement until it is understood just what it is reserves have to be sufficient for? It is almost embarrassing to ask the debaters: sufficient or insufficient for what?

A frequent answer is that international liquidity, meaning official monetary reserves plus official borrowing facilities, has been, is, or may become insufficient to "finance" a growing volume of foreign trade. No wonder that some bankers and traders engaged in international business sneer at this utterly naive justification of demands for "more liquidity." To be sure, exporters or importers with insufficient working capital may want more credit from commercial banks, domestic or foreign, but this has nothing to do with the foreign reserves of central banks or other monetary authorities. Traders with increasing volumes of international transactions may find it convenient to hold larger working balances in foreign currencies, but again this is not what is meant by international liquidity, at least not in discussions about gold and foreign-exchange reserves, supplemented by IMF reserve positions and newly created reserve assets.

A highly respected banker, not long ago, challenged anybody to produce evidence of a single international transaction that has been prevented from materializing because of a lack of international liquidity. The good man was no doubt misled by the erroneous contention that official reserves were needed for the finance of trade and payments. He had not visualized the real connection, which is this: Weak payments and reserve positions are often the reason or pretext for government policies restrictive of foreign trade and payments, and these restrictive policies prevent hundreds of thousands of international transactions — potential imports or potential foreign loans and investments — from materializing. If our challenger wanted evidence for this connection, he would only have to take it from his own files and memory — the restraints which the United States imposed on foreign lending, securities purchases, and direct investments abroad; or the surcharges which the British added in 1965 to their import duties; or the thousands of import tariffs everywhere that were introduced on "balance-of-payments grounds."

Many of the demands for the creation of additional liquidity have been "supported" by statistical data showing the declining ratio of world reserves to world trade. It is true, this ratio was 68 per cent in 1954 and fell to 37 per cent in 1966. But the decline of this ratio was the arithmetic result of an increase in trade that was faster than the increase in reserves. There is no indication that a decline in the ratio of reserves to imports when both these magnitudes are increasing has a retarding influence on trade. Even if there were a minimum or optimum ratio of reserves to imports — which we do not know — the ratio that existed in 1954 may have been so much above it that the decline in subsequent years need not have brought it down to a danger point. The only justification for placing some emphasis on the statistics of ratios of reserves to trade lies in the possibility that rising trade volumes bring with them increasing gaps between exports and imports, which would require larger reserves for the compensatory official financing of deficits. There is no evidence, however, that either the objective possibility or the subjective fear of increased trade deficits has caused or is likely to cause any retardation in the growth of trade.

There is no direct causal relationship between reserves and reserve ratios, on the one hand, and foreign-trade volumes, on the other. There is, however, an indirect connection through deliberate governmental policies. Changes in reserves or reserve ratios may influence monetary policy, fiscal policy, capital-market policy, commercial policy, incomes policy, exchange-rate policy, and so forth; and any of these policies may affect foreign trade. The first link of this causal chain, from the observed changes in the reserve position to the selected changes in policy, is fastened more likely to the changes in the *absolute* size of reserves than to changes in their *ratio* to some such other magnitude as foreign trade. A government that finds its foreign reserves increased by several per cent will not ordinarily be worried about exports and imports increasing more than foreign reserves and thus lowering the ratio of reserves to imports. The reduced ratio will not induce restrictive actions if the amount of reserves is increasing. On the other hand, an absolute loss of reserves may induce restrictive policies even if, because of a simultaneous reduction in exports and imports, the ratio of reserves to imports increases.

One should therefore be prepared to regard *changes* in official monetary reserves as more important than their absolute size, at least for most countries under most circumstances. An increase in reserves of all countries taken together, in any year, will make the gains of reserves by individual countries larger or their losses smaller. In addition, it may increase the number of countries that gain reserves and reduce the number of countries that lose reserves. As a result, these countries will be less inclined to adopt restrictive policies affecting production, employment, and trade.

One should also understand that the "need" for international reserves cannot be assessed except by judging the consequences of governmental reactions to gains or losses in reserves. The consequences of the reactions are economic in nature, but the reactions themselves are political in that they depend on the views, whims, hopes, fears, and temperaments of the men in power. One may then say that the world "needs" an increase in reserves if the (restrictive) consequences of governments reacting to losses of reserves are likely to be more harmful to world production and trade than the (expansionary) consequences of governments reacting to gains in reserves. There is no way of measuring the "need" by scientifically tested rules and formulas. After all, it is difficult to predict the distribution of deficits and surpluses in international payments and, even more, to predict the propensities of the men in power in the countries experiencing these deficits and surpluses. However, it seems clear that a world in which *many* countries suffer deficits is likely to be a rather illiberal world, with governments pursuing policies restricting imports, prohibiting capital movements, cutting down aid to poorer nations, manipulating interest rates, and controlling incomes and prices.

The Liberalizing Influence of the New System

The new system established by the Rio Agreement may, when the Governors so decide, supplement existing reserve assets by providing appropriate annual increments in the form of special drawing rights. If the combined official reserves of the participating countries are increased by, say, three billion dollars a year, their combined balances of payments will show a net surplus of three billion dollars a year. In view of the empirical correlation of illiberal policies with deficits, and of liberalization with surpluses, one may expect that the operation of the new system will have a liberalizing influence.

Since the logic of consolidated balances of payments is not always fully understood, a brief exposition of the fundamentals may be helpful at this point. To choose convenient definitions, let us say that a country has a payments *surplus* if its official reserves increase as a net result of all payments made to and received from foreign residents; and that a country has a *deficit* if its foreign transactions are such that its official reserves are reduced. If the total of official reserves of all countries together remains unchanged, no country can gain any reserve that is not lost by other countries; that is to say, the sum of all gains must equal the sum of all losses. In other words, the sum of payments surpluses must equal the sum of payments deficits. This truism, implied in the assumption of total reserves being unchanged, is sometimes mistakenly applied to a situation in which the total of reserves increases, either (as in the past) through gold acquisitions by monetary authorities or (as in the future) through the free allocation of other reserve assets. In such cases, that is, in any year in which the total of reserves increases, it is possible for some countries to gain reserves that are not lost by other countries. In any such year, the sum of payments surpluses will exceed the sum of payments deficits by the amount by which total reserves have increased.

In order to avoid an awkward snare, this statement must be qualified with regard to changes in the official holdings of reserve currencies. Official reserves are usually measured gross rather than net; thus, if the United States runs a payments deficit and finances it by increasing its official short-term liabilities to foreign monetary authorities, the statistic of gross reserves does not take account of the implicit reduction in net reserves of the United States, while it does include the addition of dollar holdings of other countries. Thus, an increase is reported in the statistic of total reserves. On the other hand, in the balance-of-payments statistic the increase in liquid liabilities of the United States is counted as reflecting a payments deficit. This asymmetry in statistical reporting explains why an increase in total reserves due to an increase in total foreign-exchange holdings is not associated with an excess of total surpluses over total deficits as they are customarily reported.

If the addition to total reserves is due to an increase in holdings of monetary gold, total surpluses exceed total deficits by the increment in monetary gold stocks. The export of new gold from gold-producing countries is part of their merchandise balance, so that these countries do not suffer a loss of reserves (financing a "deficit"); on the other hand, the import of this new gold in the receiving countries will not be treated as an import of merchandise but, instead, as an increase in reserves (financing a "surplus"). If the addition to total reserves is due to an allocation of special drawing rights, the countries will, in proper balance-of-payments accounting, enter the receipt either as long-term capital imports or as unilateral transfers (both "above the line" of the customary statement), compensated ("below the line") by the increase in official reserves that is the very purpose of the creation of SDR's.

The effect of SDR allocations upon the payments balances of the participants can be easily visualized by showing the net balances of each of the 106 member countries of the Fund in the years 1965 and 1966 and correcting them by an amount corresponding to the country's share in a total allocation. Assume, for example, that 10 per cent of the quota is distributed. Since total IMF quotas were $20,844 million at the end of 1966, the total allocation would be $2,084 million. The table in Appendix E presents the actual balances of payments in 1965 and 1966, the quotas, the 10 per cent allocations of SDR's, and the corrected surpluses and deficits. The changes resulting from the allocations are as follows.

In 1965, the combined surpluses of the 106 members of the Fund,[1] measured by increases in official gross reserves, were $4,512

---

[1] The table in Appendix E divides the 106 members (as of December 1966) into three groups. Group I is the Group of Ten, which consists really of eleven countries, since Belgium and Luxembourg are usually counted as only one member of the "Ten" but two members of the Fund. Group II includes 14 other developed countries, of which all but four — Australia, New Zealand, South Africa, and Turkey — are European. Group III, consisting of 81 developing countries, is subdivided into four sub-groups: (a) Latin America with 22 countries, (b) Middle East with 10 countries, (c) Other Asia with 15 countries, and (d) Other Africa with 34 countries. It should be noted that Indonesia rejoined the IMF only in 1967, when also The Gambia was admitted.

million and their combined deficits $3,657 million. The net surplus of $855 million must have been due to larger dollar holdings and larger IMF reserve positions of some countries. Since the Group of Ten, with a combined surplus of $2,170 million and a combined deficit of $2,142 million, had almost a zero net balance (taking all ten countries together), and the other 14 developed countries had a net deficit of $186 million, more than the total reserve increase of the entire group of 106 countries must have been earned by developing countries; indeed, the net surplus of these 81 countries was $1,013 million.

These groupings conceal significant information. The net surplus of the 81 developing countries was the result of large increases in the reserves of Brazil ($458 million), Argentina ($180 million), Saudi Arabia ($123 million), and of over 20 other countries, as against losses of reserves by the other members of this group, led by the deficit of India ($103 million). The net deficit of the 14 developed countries outside the Group of Ten includes reserve losses by ten countries, especially Australia ($358 million), South Africa ($155 million), Spain, and New Zealand, and reserve gains by only four countries. Finally, the almost perfect balance within the Group of Ten is the result of large deficits of the United States ($1,304 million), Germany ($494 million), and the United Kingdom ($344 million), offset by large surpluses of Italy ($957 million), France ($711 million), and five other countries.

Let us now see how the picture of 1965 would have been changed if, at the end of the year, SDR allocations of 10 per cent of the (1966) quota had been received by all member countries. The combined net surplus would have been raised from $855 million to some $2,900 million. The Group of Ten would have its net surplus of $28 million raised to $1,334 million. The other 14 developed countries would have their combined net deficit of $186 million changed to a net surplus of $37 million. And the 81 developing countries would have their combined net surplus increased by some $550 million.

Of real significance, of course, are only the effects on individual countries — since it is their policies that are to be influenced by the scheme. The most important result of the SDR allocation would have been that 10 of the 37 countries shown either in the deficit column or with zero balances in 1965 would have moved into the column of surplus countries. The remaining 27 would, of course, have their deficits reduced by the allocations received.

I shall not engage in all of this arithmetic exercise for 1966 but, instead, shall count the countries transformed from reserve losers to reserve gainers. There were 34 countries in the deficit column or with zero balances in 1966, and 8 of them would have moved into the surplus column if they had received allocations of SDR's of the size assumed. For a number of countries the reductions of deficits or the increases of surpluses could have had decisive influence on policy.

The "normal" reactions of governments and monetary authorities to increases in their foreign reserves are to allow "greater ease" in credit policy, fiscal policy, commercial policy, foreign lending and investment, and in foreign aid. The result is relaxation of restraints and restrictions on the demand for foreign goods, services, and securities. The liberalization that may come in the wake of the larger surpluses and smaller deficits may be merely relative, in the sense that a tightening of restrictions that would take place otherwise is averted. Even this, though, would be no small achievement.

The Inflationary Impact of the New System

If one hopes for a liberalizing influence of SDR allocations, it would be inconsistent not to expect, or perhaps to fear, an inflationary impact of the worldwide strengthening of payments and reserve positions. For, while countries may react by relaxing their restrictions on imports and other foreign payments, they may just as well react also, if not solely, by easing domestic credit.

I have considered the possibility that the relaxation may be merely relative in that otherwise imminent restrictions on trade and payments are avoided; one must likewise consider the possibility that credit restrictions that would be undertaken in order to promote real adjustment are called off in reaction to the improvement in the reserve position. In some instances, averting a restriction of credit and the deflationary consequences that it would entail may be a real blessing, both for the domestic economy and for its foreign trading partners and fund recipients. In other circumstances, however, countermanding a credit restraint designed to promote adjustment under conditions of a serious payments deficit may transform an acute situation into a chronic one, may allow national overspending to become an incorrigible practice, and may reinforce the tendency toward price and income inflations everywhere.

It is no wonder, then, that in several quarters the prospect of periodic allocations of deliberately created reserve assets is being viewed with great misgivings and outright fears about the inflationary impact of the new system. These misgivings or fears cannot, in view of all that is known of the inclinations and attitudes of central bankers, ministers, legislators, and pressure groups, be regarded as unfounded. But there is a strange inconsistency between the misgivings regarding an increase of fiduciary reserves and the sanguine reassurance regarding an increase in gold reserves. After all, the inflationary impact of an increase in gold reserves through the purchase of newly mined or dishoarded gold is faster, stronger, and more certain than that of reserve assets allocated by international fiat.

An increase in gold reserves has the following effects on the money circulation of countries that acquire them: (1) an immediate and automatic increase in the amounts of domestic money (bank deposits) first received by the corporations and individuals who were engaged in the production of the exports, the foreign-exchange proceeds of which were sold via the banks to the central bank and enabled the latter to acquire the gold; (2) an immediate and automatic increase in the domestic reserves (central-bank balances) of the commercial banks which bought the foreign exchange from exporters and sold it to the central bank; (3) an increase in the monetary reserves of the central bank (or equivalent monetary authority) that acquired the export proceeds and, with them, the gold; (4) a secondary increase in the amounts of domestic money resulting from loans and investments by commercial banks making use of the increased lending capacity provided by (2); (5) another increase of the domestic money supply and/or of the domestic reserves of commercial banks resulting from loans and investments by the central bank emboldened by the increase in its foreign reserve provided by (3); and (6) another increase of the domestic money supply resulting from loans and investments by commercial banks making use of the increased lending capacity provided by (5), the central bank's extension of credit.

This sequence of developments includes four injections of new domestic money associated with the increase in official gold reserves: (1), (4), (5), and (6). Of these (1) is completely automatic (the result of the payments surplus from private foreign transactions); (5) is entirely deliberate (the result of a central-bank decision to expand credit); (4) and (6) are based on profit-motivated credit extensions by commercial banks, the former associated with an automatic increase of their reserves, the latter with one engineered by deliberate central-bank action.

Now let me compare this with the developments to be expected from an increase in deliberately created reserves allocated to — not earned by — the participating countries. The first three automatic events do not arise; but (3), the increase in official reserves through the purchase of international money from domestic sellers, is now replaced by (3a), an increase in official reserves obtained by free allocation from the Special Drawing Account. Event (4) is again excluded. Events (5) and (6) may arise, but only if the monetary authorities decide on an expansionary policy. Thus, the sequence includes only (3a) as the direct result of the allocation, (5) the deliberate decision of the central bank, and (6) the profit-motivated credit extension by commercial banks based on the deliberate decision (5). Instead of the four injections of domestic money in the case of an increase in gold reserves, there will be only two in the case of SDR allocations, and they are not automatic.

The foregoing comparisons have focused on the initial increases in reserves, not on subsequent transfers. The effects of movements of reserves among countries will be the same whether it is gold stocks or SDR's that are transferred. Thus, if a country has a payments surplus and, therefore, "earns" more reserves, the expansionary effects will not be increased or reduced by its decision to convert the acquired foreign exchange into gold or by the decision of a deficit country to draw on the surplus country and thereby compel it to exchange foreign currency into SDR's.

The essential difference between an increase in the total gold reserves and an increase in deliberately created fiduciary reserves is that gold reserves must always be earned while allocated reserves are gratis. To earn reserves is to give up real resources in exchange; this implies an increased, and probably inflationary, foreign demand for scarce resources. To get reserves gratis means that such a foreign demand for resources is not in evidence at the time of the allocation. This is important to bear in mind if one examines the inflationary impact of the allocation of SDR's.

The Resource-Transferring Effects

Creation and allocation of SDR's do not constitute any transfer of resources among participating countries; a transfer of real resources is effected only when a country buys goods and services from another country and pays with currencies which it obtains by using some of its SDR's.

The general rule, stipulated in the Rio Agreement, says that SDR's will be used by countries for "balance-of-payments needs" to acquire convertible currencies from countries with "a sufficiently strong balance-of-payments and reserve position." If one could assume that these deficits and surpluses exist in given amounts, independent of the availability of SDR's, then one might conclude that the resource-transferring effects of the use of SDR's cannot be significant. The use of SDR's would merely replenish the currency reserves of deficit countries and drain off some of the currency accruals of surplus countries. But, of course, the assumption would be quite unrealistic. There is little doubt that the availability of the new reserve assets will affect some countries' policies, which in turn will result in deficits and surpluses that would not have existed, or would have been smaller, without the allocation of additional reserves.

The resource-transferring effects, indirect but possibly significant, of the creation of SDR's will be seen in the larger magnitude and/or longer duration of payments deficits of countries that are encouraged by their improved reserve position to pursue policies promoting the demand for imports of goods, services, or securities. These may be policies of relaxing restrictions on imports and on foreign lending and investing, or of increasing effective demand by easing credit and fiscal policies. In either case, payments deficits may be created or increased, which can then be financed, at least in part, by the use of SDR's.

The transfer of real resources is, of course, from surplus countries to deficit countries. This does not necessarily mean that the countries that are "drawn upon" by users of SDR's are actually the ones that are giving up resources. It is possible that deficit countries purchase their "excess" imports from countries that have not yet accumulated reserve positions strong enough to be selected for drawings, and that the drawings are made upon countries not "enjoying" or "suffering" (according to the point of view) the payments surpluses which imply surrender of real resources. These countries will then have given up convertible currencies, but no real resources, in exchange for SDR's. The countries contributing real resources for use by the deficit countries (or for use by countries receiving grants, loans, or investments from the deficit countries) would then be paid in convertible currencies, not in SDR's. This ought to be borne in mind, lest one mistakes the excess holders of SDR's always for the contributors of the real resources transferred to the deficit countries.

It is one of the maxims or canons of liquidity creation that it ought not to lead to unrequited, long-run transfers of resources. The creation of new reserves should facilitate merely temporary transfers of resources by helping to finance swings in payments balances, without forcing the participating countries to use unduly restrictive measures for the purpose of getting a larger share in an inadequate total of reserves. In the long run, however, the distribution of SDR's, as well as of other reserves, is not supposed to change drastically. A lasting redistribution of reserves would mean that the net users of reserves have drawn real resources from net accumulators of reserves, in disregard of the announced principles of the system.

Few observers have illusions about the observance of these principles. The negotiating parties were realistic enough not to hold the participating countries to an excessively strict regimen in the use of SDR's. Stern demands by some negotiators for a rule of reconstituting 50 per cent of allocated balances within relatively short periods were eventually softened to the rule of reconstituting an average balance of only 30 per cent over a five-year period. This does allow for a net use of 70 per cent of the allocated amounts for five years, hence, for using the scheme to get hold of other countries' resources for more than brief intervals. Of course, if the annual allocations are not large, even a most immoderate use of them by some of the countries cannot give the users intolerably large claims to the resources of their partners.

Misgivings regarding the possibility that the provision of additional liquidity may be misused by some countries to secure for themselves quasi-permanent access to real resources of other countries have been expressed repeatedly.[2] Less-developed countries, chronic-deficit countries, and reserve-currency countries have been seen in the role of potential filchers of their neighbors' wealth by spending instead of holding the new monetary reserves. I shall later examine these three groups of countries suspected of a propensity to spend as much as they can and thus to impose on others the role of involuntary benefactors.

To Whom Shall Be Given?

In the years of debate, several alternative solutions to the problem of international liquidity had been proposed, disputed, defended, and rejected. One of the important questions was whether the new international purchasing power should be put at the disposal of a particular group of countries — such as the poor, the rich, the conservative, or the broke ones (if we may suggest these irreverent

---

2 "We are agreed that deliberate reserve creation is not intended to effect permanent transfers of real resources from some countries to others." "Report to the Ministers and Governors by the Group of Deputies," July 7, 1966 [Otmar Emminger, Chairman] in *Communiqué of Ministers and Governors and Report of Deputies,* Group of Ten, July 1966, §40. (Note: This Report will hereafter be cited as the Emminger Report.)

characterizations of the intended first beneficiaries of the various plans proposed) — or whether it should be distributed to all countries "across the board."

To give the new "liquidity" first to poor countries was the idea of those who wanted to attain two objectives with one action by creating new reserves in the process of aiding less-developed countries. The best-known plan of this sort was that proposed by Maxwell Stamp.[3] An expanded IMF was to issue certificates to the International Development Association; this organization would distribute the certificates to developing countries, which would use them for purchases from any industrial countries that are prepared to accept them as part of their monetary reserves. The industrial countries, therefore, would earn additional reserves by exports to developing countries using the new money.

The Triffin Plan included the same possibility along with other reserve-creating techniques. It provided for open-market purchases of securities by the extended IMF or any other organization operating like a supranational reserve bank.[4] The securities acquired in the process of creating "credit reserves" could include International Bank for Reconstruction and Development (IBRD) bonds or other obligations of development-finance organizations; in providing a broader market for such securities, the creation of additional reserves would contribute financial aid to poor countries.

One of the several plans proposed by Sir Roy Harrod would have aided developing countries in their capacity as producers and exporters of primary commodities.[5] The scheme was to create new international money — deposits with the IMF — in the process of financing large buffer-stock operations designed to secure stable prices to the exporters of primary products. The new money would be put into circulation by an International Buffer Stock Authority

---

[3] For a brief description, see Fritz Machlup, *Plans for Reform of the International Monetary System* (Princeton: International Finance Section, revised edition 1964), pp. 47-49.

[4] *Ibid.*, pp. 45-46, and 50.

[5] *Ibid.*, p. 54.

paying for commodities purchased at stipulated support prices from the producing countries.

An official proposal for investments by the IMF "in an instrument issued by the IBRD" was recorded in the Ossola Report of 1965. The "beneficiaries" would use the currencies distributed by the IBRD "for purchases from industrialized countries and additional assets [currencies] would thus find their way into the reserves of countries which were in surplus."[6]

Most members of the Group of Ten, however, did not favor "coupling" the two "quite distinct" objectives of adding international liquidity and aiding developing countries. They saw the problem of reserve assets as one of concern mainly to the 11 financially advanced countries — the Ten plus Switzerland — which in December 1964 held 72.6 per cent of the monetary reserves of the free world. Many of the techniques of reserve creation which they considered were envisaged as creating reserves exclusively for themselves. Since the ten countries were among the richest of the world, the Group was quickly dubbed a Rich-Man's Club; and the idea of creating new reserve assets for the monetary authorities of the Ten was characterized as a case of "to him who hath shall be given."

Foremost among such plans for closely held new reserves was the proposal to create Collective Reserve Units (CRU's). These were defined as "assets, created outside the IMF by a limited group of industrial countries, in agreed amounts, from time to time" upon unanimous decision by the group.[7] The French proposal favored a procedure of "crossed deposits in gold"— each participant depositing gold with a central Agent, and the Agent "in turn" depositing the same amount of gold with each participant — so that the CRU's would be "distributed to participants in proportion to their gold reserves."[8]

---

[6] *Report of the Study Group on the Creation of Reserve Assets: Report to the Deputies of the Group of Ten*, May 31, 1965 [Rinaldo Ossola, Chairman] published August 1965, §137. (Note: This Report will hereafter be cited as the Ossola Report.)

[7] *Ibid.*, §§28 and 30.

[8] *Ibid.*, §§31 and 33, also §49(a).

This plan was strongly opposed by other members of the Group of Ten, on the ground that it "would be inequitable and would introduce an incentive to maximize gold at the expense of other reserves" and, moreover, "would represent a disguised increase in the gold price for the countries concerned and would induce speculation in gold markets."[9] But, although this formula for distributing the new reserve asset was rejected, there was still strong sentiment among the deliberating and negotiating officials for schemes that would keep the new asset among the small group of ten or eleven countries.

The idea of creating a new reserve asset for only the rich countries was of course never put forth as a self-serving one; nor was it really intended to be a selfish and ungenerous scheme. The conception, instead, rested on the propositions (1) that a new reserve asset would be acceptable only if it were supported by the credit of the financially responsible countries and (2) that new reserves should be created only for those who could be expected to hold them rather than to spend them. In line with the latter proposition one may, stressing an alternative principle of selecting the recipients of additional reserves, regard plans of this sort as schemes of giving the new money to the conservative. Conservative in this context are countries that have a record of holding large amounts of monetary reserves relative to their imports and of treating additions to reserves as something to hold on to rather than to dissipate.

Even as late as July 1966 the Ministers and Central Bank Governors of the Ten stressed, as an important principle of any future arrangements, "the particular responsibilities of a limited group of major countries with a key role in the functioning of the international monetary system." The Report of the Deputies, appended to their Communiqué, recited several reasons for limiting the group of participants in a scheme of reserve creation either to the ten countries or to a few more with "agreed qualifications" (but "the Group should not be too large").[10]

---

[9] *Ibid.*, §159(a) and (e), also §116.

[10] Emminger Report, *op. cit.*, §§58-62.

Four of the five schemes described in the "Annex" to the 1966 Report of the Deputies proposed creation of reserve units or of special reserve drawing rights by a "limited group," and only one scheme offered participation to all members of the Fund.

Creation of international liquidity, not for the conservative countries but, on the contrary, for countries unable otherwise to meet their payments deficits, is the one distribution that the Group of Ten rejected repeatedly and explicitly. Although some wiseacres insisted that money was needed neither by the rich nor by the conservative but really only by the broke, the Ten had agreed that the creation of liquidity "should be neither geared nor directed to the financing of balance-of-payments deficits of individual countries."[11]

This agreement, though presumably unanimous, was contradicted by proposals, emanating from within the Group of Ten, that credit facilities for those who wanted loans would, after all, be the soundest way of meeting the problem of international liquidity. The contradiction, between the extension of credits to countries in weak payments and reserve positions and the principle of making the creation of reserves independent of the deficits of individual countries, was perhaps not completely understood by some. Or, maybe, they changed their minds and thought that, since allocations to all countries "across the board" would help the poor and the broke along with the rich and conservative, it might be wiser to deal with the would-be spenders in a forthright fashion, discuss with them as would-be borrowers their situation, policies, and intentions; and grant them credit if they deserved it.

Partiality versus Universality

We know, of course, that the principle of "universality"— giving to all — was eventually adopted in preference to any of the systems implying partiality to any group of countries. However, lest I en-

---

11 "Communiqué of the Ministerial Meeting of the Group of Ten," July 25 and 26, 1966, at The Hague, in *Communiqué of Ministers and Governors and Report of Deputies,* Group of Ten, July 1966. Similar statements appeared in the reports of 1964 and 1965.

courage unthinking and scornful condemnation of all proposals for selective distributions, I should like to pay some attention to the arguments with which the discriminatory schemes were defended or criticized.

Partiality for poor countries is easy to understand. Against the puristic demand for clean separation of the need for monetary reserves in the entire world and the need for capital for development in individual countries, political expediency was claimed in favor of "combining asset creation with development finance." It is often difficult for governments of the more affluent countries to obtain legislative approval for the development aid that they deem wise and proper to extend. By giving the aid in an indirect, less overt fashion, burdening neither the governmental budget nor the balance of payments, a difficult and controversial procedure is replaced by a painless, sometimes even pleasant process. The countries can avoid parliamentary fights for appropriations, fiscal agonies about budget deficits, irksome tensions in capital markets, and nasty problems concerning foreign payments deficits; the only manifestations of their indirect aid to poor countries would be increases in exports and inflows of monetary reserves.

Another argument stresses considerations of equity and fairness; discrimination in favor of developing countries in the distribution of new reserves should be considered acceptable as a compensatory bonus for the discrimination against developing countries that is inherent in the process of adjustment as it operates to restore balance in international payments. On theoretical grounds it is argued that the burden of adjustment, in the form of the sacrifices imposed on the economy in the process of resource reallocation, is relatively much heavier on the poor countries which specialize in production and export of primary commodities. Partiality in the allocation of monetary reserves would be a partial compensation for the unequal incidence of the cost of adjustment, in that the less-developed countries would be enabled to purchase some of the additional imports required to make good the losses suffered through the reallocation of real resources in the adjustment process.

A third argument points to the fact that the proposed discrimination in favor of poor countries would not impose any new or added burden on the industrial countries. If the latter have been and are still willing to buy gold supplied by South African or Russian gold mines and, thus, to earn such increases in the monetary reserves through deliveries of net exports, that is, by letting some other country have products of their real resources, they should not mind earning some "paper gold" in exactly the same way. Fiduciary reserves can serve the same purpose as gold reserves; hence, countries willing to earn gold reserves through export surpluses should be no less willing to earn fiduciary reserves in the same fashion. To be sure, the paper and the ink used to print or record claims to other nations' currencies (and, indirectly, to other nations' real resources) cost almost nothing; and one can understand that the industrial countries dislike the thought of having to pay for international money that can be created without cost the same price, in terms of exports, as for international commodity money that has to be dug out of the bowels of the earth and refined in costly processes. But the point is that the benefit from creating costless money rather than costly money must accrue to someone, and who should be the beneficiary is necessarily an arbitrary decision.

The following consideration may be of help in evaluating the proposals partial to the poor countries. Under the gold standard, industrial countries earned increases in their gold reserves through exports to South Africa; workers in mines and refining plants (and, of course, also managers and stockholders) received the equivalent of what the industrial countries exported in exchange for the gold. Under a system of allocating fiduciary international money to developing countries, industrial countries would earn these new reserve assets through exports to any of the developing countries that spend the allocated money; workers in development projects, such as in the construction of highways, schools, or hospitals, would receive goods and services equivalent to the industrial countries' exports. The effects on the industrial countries would be the same in both cases; the effects on the developing countries would differ in that the development projects may sooner or later help to increase the productivity of their people.

Partiality toward rich countries may look much less appealing, but can be defended on several grounds. For example, one may say that most or all of the newly created reserves would be held by a small group of industrially and financially advanced countries, and no country outside this group would suffer any loss by the limited group's creating their own "chips." The rich countries would either add the new reserve assets to their idle (inactive) holdings or use them exclusively among themselves for settling temporary intra-group imbalances; neither of these results would affect the outsiders in any respect.

As one of the (French) arguments for the Collective Reserve Unit (CRU), it was said that "limiting membership in the scheme to a small and homogeneous group of industrial countries would be justified by the special reserve needs of such countries."[12] This notion of "special needs" was linked with one concerning "management problems." It was argued that "the formation of judgments" would "only be likely to succeed in practice within a group of limited size and homogeneous composition."[13] Such exclusivity would "facilitate decision-making and would avoid the problems arising from the participation of persistent debtors."[14]

Finally, "in favor of keeping the ownership and circulation of the asset within a limited group of industrialized countries, it was argued that an international asset must be based on credit and that the credit of those who back it must therefore be unquestioned."[15] This has probably been the strongest talking-point in favor of limit-

---

[12] Ossola Report, op cit., §158(b). The same report, in §118, explained more specifically that "the needs of the larger industrialized countries which share the responsibility for the working of the international monetary system are different not only in scale but in kind from those of the rest of the world. These are the countries which principally hold and use reserves for international monetary purposes; and their reserve needs are a primary concern of the international system."

[13] Ibid., §118.

[14] Ibid., §158(b).

[15] Ibid., §120.

ing the reserve creation to a group of rich countries.[16] In one form or another this argument was maintained until the last stages of the negotiations — though it had to be given up in the end.

The defense of partiality toward conservative countries emphasized the sound or cautious monetary and fiscal policies of countries determined to maintain safe reserve positions and to take prompt adjustment measures whenever a payments deficit arises or threatens to arise. The virtue of such conservative practices has always been praised in textbooks and official speeches everywhere and, thus, proposals to limit schemes of reserve creation to the small company of virtuous countries could win wide acceptance among the virtuous, and particularly among reformed sinners.

Advocates of this exclusivity claimed that care was needed "in establishing the group" in which reserve assets were to be used. "A reserve asset is characterized by the expectation that, if it flows out, it should ordinarily be reconstituted in due time. Assets which are specifically created to fulfill the reserve function should, consequently, be distributed only to countries whose balance of payments is likely to move between deficit and surplus and which are, therefore, able to assume the obligations as well as the rights entailed in the convention and its working."[17]

It was obvious to everybody that not all the rich were virtuous, and not all the virtuous were rich. Hence, the group of countries eligible to participate in a scheme of deliberate creation of international liquidity would have to be determined by their qualifications. If a good "balance-of-payments record" is regarded as the main criterion of eligibility, several poor countries could qualify. Indeed, "a number of the smaller countries could show that they have maintained a good reserve position and that their balance-of-

---

[16] See also the section on "Participation" in the July 1966 Report of the Group of Deputies. Among the arguments listed in favor of limiting the creation of reserve assets to the Group of Ten were that "full acceptance" of these assets "requires that they be backed by major trading and financial countries," and that countries would find these assets "more convincing as a supplement to gold" if they "were created by a limited group of countries which together hold a substantial amount of gold." Emminger Report, *op. cit.*, §§56-62.

[17] Ossola Report, *op. cit.*, §120.

payments record compares favorably with that of countries within the group [of Ten]."[18]

Another set of criteria of eligibility to join a "limited but open-ended group" of participants was proposed in "Scheme A," appended to the 1966 Report of the Deputies of the Group of Ten. It consisted in the assumption of certain obligations, including those of "multilateral surveillance" and of abiding by rules to be prescribed in an agreement on the adjustment process. Thus, admission to the exclusive group would not depend on the record of correct conduct in the past, but rather on solemn promises of good behavior in the future.

Those who want countries to be subjected to greater "balance-of-payments discipline" have usually advocated reserve creation through extension of conditional credits to countries forced to borrow in order to meet their payments deficits. By lending to the broke ones, on conditions guaranteeing good behavior regarding adjustment and early repayment of the loans, the new reserves accrue to countries that have earned them through their exports to the deficit countries.

Two arguments have been advanced against the advocacy of reserve creation through credits to countries in financial straits. One argument points to the inclination of these countries to avoid both the financing through short-term borrowing and the adjustments through monetary and fiscal restraint, and to attempt instead to correct their payments position through restrictions on imports and capital outflows. The other argument stresses the unreliability of the growth of total reserves and the instability of the volume of reserves if the demand for new loans determines the growth of reserves and if net repayments of old loans may at any time reduce the volume of reserves.[19]

Thus, one can see that reasonable arguments can be mustered in support of, as well as in opposition to, any one of the plans for giving new international means of payment to particular groups of

---

[18] *Ibid.*, §121.

[19] These arguments will be discussed later in greater detail.

countries. After years of discussion, the defenses of partiality were abandoned and the principle of universality, of allocations to all Fund members that want to participate, was adopted.

Some spokesmen for universal and unconditional eligibility have formulated arguments to justify the adoption of this principle. They have mentioned the resentment of discrimination; the consequent harm to international cooperation; the fact that all countries, not only a selected few, need increasing amounts of monetary reserves; and the unfairness of forcing some of them, probably the poorest, to earn their additional reserves while others get the unearned increments under an exclusive deal. Some of those who initially had favored some sort of partiality have finally accepted the principle of universality, because they realized that the arguments for particular schemes of exclusivity were, by and large, weaker than the counter-arguments, and that the disadvantages or risks of universal participation were relatively small compared with the possible consequences of discriminatory solutions.

Scuttling the Myth of "Backing"

To reject partiality toward the rich countries is only to reject the demand that new reserve assets be allocated exclusively to the rich; it need not imply rejection of the offer of the rich nations to "back" the new reserves with their superior financial power and creditworthiness. This offer has repeatedly been made but, in the end, it was rejected too.

In several of the schemes discussed by the Deputies of the Group of Ten, allocation to *all,* but backing by the *few* had been proposed. Backing by the "major" countries was considered essential for success of any scheme and it was taken for granted that this meant backing *exclusively* by these countries, chiefly in the form of deposits of their currencies or securities. As a corollary of providing these collateral deposits, the pledging countries expected to be accorded special voting and vetoing rights.

The notion of backing is associated with the notion of debt-money. The issuer of the debts (certificates, notes, or deposit liabilities) which circulate as money is supposed to hold good assets against the circulating liabilities, and the quality of the assets is believed to be a necessary condition of the moneyness (that is, acceptability) of the liabilities. Since the assets "behind" the debt-money are ordinarily debts of some financially respectable and credit-worthy persons, corporations, or countries, the theoretical link between the quality of the ultimate debtors (backers), the quality of the assets (backing), and the acceptability of the immediate debt (money) seems to be established. This venerable myth has long enjoyed wide currency, especially in banking circles.

Practically all the plans and schemes for the creation of new international liquidity had incorporated these notions. There was to be a central legal debtor — the IMF, BIS, or a new international institution — and the certificates or deposit liabilities of this legal debtor (or drawing rights against this legal debtor) were to be backed by the currencies or securities of the debtor's debtors — the financially responsible countries.

The new facility established by the Rio Agreement dispenses with the central legal debtor of the special drawing rights and, of course, with the debtor's debtors. By implication, it disposes of the old myth of backing. In so doing, the officials of the Fund and of the negotiating governments showed a courage far greater than the academic economists have had. Not that any reputable economist of our time has believed the old myth; but they were convinced that all bankers and other practical men of the world of finance believed in the myth and could not possibly be "enlightened." Thus, the academic economists had not dared to recommend schemes that would do away with the trappings of backing. Now the forward-looking experts of the Fund and the negotiating governments have proved that their reputation for backwardness in economic thinking had been undeserved. (I propose that they be granted honorary doctor's degrees by the great universities.)

All that matters for the acceptability of anything as a medium of exchange is the expectation that others will accept it. If over a hundred central banks or national monetary authorities including those of the major trading nations of the world agree to accept SDR's from one another in exchange for convertible currencies, this is all that is needed to establish the moneyness of the SDR's in inter-central-bank transactions. Money needs takers, not backers; the takers accept it, not because of any backing, but only because they count on others accepting it from them.

The myth of backing is dead. It was buried in Rio de Janeiro on September 29, 1967.

A Boon for Less-Developed Countries?

The principle of universality in the distribution of new drawing rights had been opposed, as I have noted, partly because it involved giving financial aid to developing countries which would not hold increased reserves but rather spend their entire allocations. Now that it is agreed that the less-developed countries will participate in all allocations, one may ask how much help these countries may expect from the new system when it goes into operation.

Let us assume, for purposes of illustration and for the sake of simplicity, that in the first year SDR's in an amount of 10 per cent of Fund quotas will be allocated, which is a little more than $2 billion. How much would go to developing countries? How much of this could they spend if they decided, in conformance with the rule regarding the five-year "net average use," to hold 30 per cent of the allocated amounts as a minimum balance? How much would their additional spending power be in relation to their recent balances of payments, their total imports, their national incomes, their capital imports?

Answers to some of these questions can be read off the table in Appendix E. The developing countries of Latin America, Africa, the Middle East and the rest of Asia would receive $556 million of a total allocation of $2,084 million. If they kept 30 per cent, they would have an extra $389 million to spend. Their consolidated balance of payments in 1966 showed a net surplus of $812 million. If, over and above this figure, they would have received $556 million as an allocation of SDR's and spent none of it, their combined net additions to reserves would have been increased to $1,368 million. If they had immediately (which, however, is not a very realistic assumption) spent $389 million of the new funds, they would still have had a combined net surplus of $979 million.

Of greater interest is the relation of the new spending power to the other global magnitudes of the developing countries. Their total imports in 1966 were $39,760 million. Hence, 70 per cent of the SDR's allocated would allow an increase of these imports by less than one per cent. The combined gross domestic product of developing countries was $321 billion in 1966 (which is a rather unreliable estimate, of course). The use of $389 million in SDR's would imply an increase in outlays for consumption and home investment of one-tenth of one per cent of their gross domestic product. Capital imports — long-term capital and donations — in 1965 were $8.9 billion. The 70 per cent of the SDR allocation would be 4.4 per cent of such capital imports.

If some or all of these figures may be disappointing to those who expected that the developing countries would obtain substantial aid from the allocation of new reserves, a few additional reflections may aggravate or alleviate the disappointment.

A target has often been set for the financial aid which the developed part of the world ought to give to the undeveloped part. This target was one per cent of the gross national product of the developed countries. Taking account only of the noncommunist countries, the target aid would, on the basis of 1966 figures, amount to $11.8 billion. The SDR allocations to developing countries, of the size assumed, would be 3.3 per cent of the target aid, not a really significant contribution.

Of course, reserves are not designed to be used for meeting long-term capital needs. As countries develop, they will want to have their foreign reserves grow at some rate (even if the rate is below that of the growth of production, trade, and domestic money supply). It will be a welcome relief if the developing countries obtain the desired increments in foreign reserves without having to earn them, that is, if their attempts to build up reserves need not be at the expense of capital investment in productive facilities.

The most important benefit that the new facility may confer upon less-developed countries is not a direct one, however. It may come through changes in aid policies and in commercial policies on the part of industrial countries. This theme has been presented in earlier sections of this essay and needs no further development or recapitulation. A reminder should suffice. Improvements in the payments and reserve positions of the more affluent nations may allow these nations to relax some of their present restrictions on imports and foreign aid. The effects on their demand for imports and on their supply of capital funds may mean much more for the development efforts of poor countries than any direct aid these countries can receive through the allocation of special drawing rights.

Once more: the benefits which the less-developed countries may obtain through additional trade and additional aid made possible through SDR allocations to developed countries may be much greater than any direct benefits through SDR allocations to them.

A Boon for Chronic-Deficit Countries?

Some of the governments in the Group of Ten have been greatly concerned about the help which the deliberate creation of reserves would afford to countries in chronic deficit. They warned that reserve creation would "weaken the incentive for countries to take measures to restore equilibrium in their balance of payments"[20] and "would open the way to the additional financing of deficits."[21] Indeed, one government (evidently the French) had long resisted the "drafting of an international agreement for the deliberate creation of reserves" lest it "give rise to an irresistible temptation to activate the agreement prematurely"; efforts of some countries to eliminate their deficits "would be hampered by the presumed availability of new financing facilities."[22]

The same government, through M. Debré, reminded the Governors of the Fund assembled in Rio that the new "mechanism cannot come into play until there is a more satisfactory operation of the existing adjustment processes" and until the payments deficits of the reserve-currency countries "have disappeared." Secretary

---

[20] Ossola Report, *op. cit.*, §153(b).
[21] *Ibid.*, §154(b) (though this paragraph relates to a different scheme).
[22] Emminger Report, *op. cit.*, §46(c) and (d).

Fowler, of the United States, likewise recalled the 1966 Agreement of the Group of Ten to the effect that "attainment of a better balance-of-payments equilibrium between members and the likelihood of a better working of the adjustment process in the future" were among the prerequisites for the activation of the scheme. Thus, "the new facility . . . is not designed to meet the problems of an individual country's balance-of-payments problem." [The speaker of this sentence must have had quite a problem with "the problems of the problem."]

If M. Debré's version is strictly observed, then the creation of SDR's cannot be any aid to the notorious "chronic-deficit countries," because their deficits must "have disappeared" before activation of the scheme. If Mr. Fowler's version is observed, and a "better equilibrium" need not mean full balance, then the decision for activation may come before the deficits have completely disappeared. In this case, the allocation to the United States may turn out to be, even if it is not designed to be, a contribution to the financing of its deficit.

In view of this possibility, it may be interesting to compare the recent payments deficits of the United States and United Kingdom with the first allocations in the amounts previously assumed for purposes of illustration. These allocations, of 10 per cent of the Fund quota, would be $516 million for the United States and $244 million for the United Kingdom. On the basis of official settlements (that is, disregarding changes in liquid liabilities to nonofficial creditors) the United States had a deficit of $1,304 million in 1965, a freak surplus of $225 million in 1966, and a deficit (at a preliminary figure) of $3,400 million in 1967. The United Kingdom had a deficit of $344 million in 1965, and a deficit of $1,567 million in 1966. Allocations of SDR's in the assumed amounts would have accomplished the following changes:

United States, 1965, deficit of $1,304 million reduced to $788 million,

United States, 1966, surplus of $225 million increased to $741 million,

United Kingdom, 1965, deficit of $344 million reduced to $100 million,

United Kingdom, 1966, deficit of $1,567 million reduced to $1,323 million.

One may well differ in one's judgment on whether these changes would mean much for the positions and policies of the two countries. I am inclined to give more weight to the development of reserve positions and their changes for a *longer* period of years. The United Kingdom, having experienced its periodic balance-of-payments crises for more than 18 years and being confronted with a position of extreme illiquidity at the moment, would hardly find that the SDR allocations in the amount assumed here constituted sufficient relief to justify a change from a policy of restraint to a policy of ease. The United States, having had only three years with surpluses in its balance of official settlements since 1950, and only one year with a surplus in its liquidity balance, and having lost almost 50 per cent of its gold reserve, would not be likely to be swayed by the receipt of drawing rights amounting to less than 5 per cent of that loss of gold. Both countries would surely appreciate any relief that could improve their reserve position or retard its deterioration, and this might make a difference regarding some specific short-run policies. But one may doubt that their long-run fiscal and monetary policies would be fundamentally affected by the relief directly implied in the receipt of reserve allocations in the order of magnitude here considered.

All this, however, is not very important in comparison with the indirect benefits to countries in potentially chronic deficit and, one step removed, to virtually all countries trading with them or aided by them. In an attempt to explain the interdependences involved in the network of international payments, we shall confine ourselves to the United States as the chronic-deficit country *par excellence*.

Assume that, in conformance with French intransigence, no SDR's are created so long as the United States runs a deficit in its international payments. Assume further that, as has been the case for almost three years, no new gold becomes available for monetary reserves. Assume finally that all countries but the United States pursue policies designed to secure them increases in their monetary reserves of, say, 3 per cent per year on the average. (Total reserves of all Fund members except the United States were some $57 billion at the end of 1966; 3 per cent of this is $1.7 billion.) Now it follows from the stated assumptions that these reserve aspirations can succeed only if the United States has a deficit of $1.7 billion. And this is true whether other countries are prepared to hold increasing amounts of dollars or whether they insist on taking their surplus in the form of gold. In either case, only a deficit of the United States can make it possible for the rest of the world to increase their reserves (without new supplies of gold and without creation of SDR's).

If the United States is to avoid this deficit, it can do so only by defeating the efforts of other countries to have surpluses in their balances of payments. To defeat these efforts the United States would have to take very drastic measures of a restrictive nature: restrictive of military expenditures abroad, restrictive of foreign aid, restrictive of capital exports, restrictive of imports, restrictive of domestic credit, and, last but not least, restrictive of domestic employment and growth. These measures, of course, can succeed only to the extent that other nations acquiesce in being frustrated in their own desires with regard to trade, capital movements, and payments and reserve positions. Many of these countries are likely to defend their positions by embarking on equally restrictive policies and thereby again imposing a deficit on the United States that alone is consistent with the attainment of the other countries' national objectives.

The only way out of this vicious circle is to escape from one of our assumptions. It would be difficult to change the third assumption, the attitudes.of the leaders of most countries — attitudes that have had the approval of political economists from the days of mercantilism to our times of neo-mercantilism (that is, chiefly, a determination to secure national economic growth and full employment even at the cost of unneighborly restrictions and controls). It would be silly to alter the second assumption, the conditions of gold supply. But it should be possible to persuade the required majority of countries to activate the scheme for deliberate creation of monetary reserves in the form of special drawing rights *before* the United States has eliminated its payments deficit.

If enough reserves are created to satisfy the other countries' national objectives regarding their payments and reserve positions without imposing a deficit on the United States, this deficit would have at least a chance to disappear. In this sense, the allocations of reserve assets would benefit the country with the potentially chronic deficit and, in the process, would benefit the rest of the world by allowing universal disarmament in the economic warfare for "satisfactory" reserve positions.

The argument just presented is vulnerable to charges of exaggeration and oversimplification. Critics may object to a simplistic exposition that invites misinterpretation to the effect that the United States has in unselfish generosity pursued policies to accommodate other countries' desires for surpluses in their balances of payments. This, however, was neither said nor meant. The argument merely pointed to the fact that the other countries' policies designed to achieve surpluses could succeed only to the extent that the United States acquiesced in a commensurate deficit.

The charge of exaggeration may be supported by a denial of the assumption that most countries actually are so hepped on having surpluses year after year. Of course not. In the last few years, Italy and Germany have occasionally had large deficits. Yes, but would they, or other countries, acquiesce in such deficits if they were not sure that the long-run trend of their reserves was upward? Measures to stop deficits and get back into surplus positions are "prescribed" by all the manuals on the adjustment process. Several countries are periodically admonished to build up their reserves, but no country is told (or tells others) that it should (or would) create a payments deficit in order to reduce its reserves. This adds up to a confirmation of the assumption that the non-dollar world desires a net surplus in its payments. And this is consistent only with deficits of the United States — unless the world can have an aggregate net surplus through the creation of additional reserves.

A Boon for Reserve-Currency Countries?

The fact that the United States and the United Kingdom are chronic-deficit countries as well as reserve-currency countries may seem to make a separate discussion of their latter role unnecessary (particularly so because only a country with a currency that serves as a monetary reserve for other countries can finance a large chronic deficit). Yet, the subject of discussion in this section is different. It is independent of any deficits of the reserve-currency countries. It concerns the possibility of switches among different reserve assets held by monetary authorities and of the consequences which such demands for conversion may have for the countries concerned and for the system as a whole.

The amounts of United States dollars and United Kingdom pounds held in the official reserves of Fund members are more than 30 per cent of total reserves. (Total reserves on September 30, 1967, were $72 billion, of which $16.4 billion were in dollars and $7.5 billion in pounds.) The percentage of foreign-exchange reserves in the reserves of all countries *other* than the two reserve-currency countries is, of course, still larger.

One of the most pressing problems of our time has been the possibility that the holders of these reserves may decide to convert large portions of them into gold. Since the United States in December 1967 had only $12.1 billion, and the United Kingdom only an estimated $1.8 billion of monetary gold, it would obviously be impossible to convert all official holdings of dollars and pounds into gold. But even an attempt at any large-scale conversion may have very serious consequences, particularly in view of the fact that there exist also vast private holdings of these currencies, chiefly in the form of working balances of private banks and traders. Sudden crises of confidence could, quite apart from the disruption of financial markets, lead to deflationary spirals with disastrous effects on employment and production in many countries.

This so-called problem of "confidence" or "stability" — neither term is really descriptive — has been well known to economists and officials. Numerous plans for treating the problem have been proposed and discussed for years. The question whether the Rio Agreement contributes to the solution must, unfortunately, be answered negatively. Two types of solution had been considered in the course of the negotiations: (1) exchanging unwanted holdings of dollars or pounds into claims against the Fund (the IMF becoming an intermediary between debtors and creditors), or (2) locking-in the existing foreign-exchange holdings in the reserves of the various monetary authorities by "harmonization rules" (committing the participants to hold certain minimum portions of their reserves in the form of the currencies in question). Both types of solution were rejected by at least one country and the problem was left largely unsolved.

Certain provisions of the Outline may yet contribute tangentially to the prevention of foreseeable demands for conversion. For example, the provision which allows a participating country to use its SDR's "to purchase balances of its currency held by another participant, with the agreement of the latter" [V, 3, (d)] would enable the United States to offer SDR's to a country that otherwise would use dollar balances for conversion into gold.

A rather indirect alleviation of the conversion problem may be expected if the activation of the plan, creating a reserve asset that substitutes for increases in monetary gold stocks, changes the speculative climate and reduces the private demand for gold. Without speculative purchases of gold, there would be some excess supply from new production and accumulated hoards available for acquisition by monetary authorities.

These tangentially or indirectly helpful effects on the conversion problem are entirely inadequate to safeguard the international monetary system against serious disturbances. Neither the Executive Directors of the Fund nor the Ministers and Governors of the Group of Ten should be allowed to rest on their laurels. They deserve laurels for what they have achieved regarding the problem of liquidity. But they do not deserve any rest until they have solved the problem of confidence in the existing reserve currencies. Indeed, they should not lose much time — for there may not be much time before the problem becomes another crisis.[23]

---

[23] This was written in October 1967, several weeks before the crisis of the pound sterling that led to its devaluation. The statements in the text remain relevant.

Development, Adjustment, Confidence, and Liquidity

Lest the reader has failed to notice the logic in the sequence of this discussion, it may be well to point out how the focus of my analysis has, in the last three sections, moved from the problem of liquidity to three collateral problems, all separate and yet inter-dependent: development, adjustment, and confidence.

The connections among the four problems are manifold. To discuss them here would go too far beyond the scope of this essay; but to allude to them briefly may help one avoid disorientation.

To create additional liquidity for the nations of this world is to allow some of them to draw on the real resources of others, temporarily — for periods short or long — or even "for good." Nations in need of capital for development purposes will not easily resist the temptation to use the new funds, which are meant to provide liquid reserves, to finance permanent additions to their productive facilities. Thus, a facility to furnish liquidity may, in contradiction to the accepted design, furnish development aid.

To create additional liquidity is to allow some countries to postpone the adjustment or corrective measures that can eliminate payments deficits. If these countries are unwilling to tolerate real adjustment (devaluation or deflation) and would resort only to correctives of a restrictive character (import barriers, capital re-straints, exchange controls), the use of new liquidity for the con-tinued finance of payments deficits may obstruct the obstruction of trade and payments — but cannot be responsible for blocking a real adjustment that is ruled out in any case. However, this state of affairs is intolerable in the long run; an international code on the working of the adjustment mechanism will have to be formulated and agreed upon.

To create additional liquidity is not, alas, to forestall crises of confidence in existing reserve assets. Attempts by large official holders of dollars or pounds to have these reserve currencies con-verted into gold may destroy large amounts of monetary reserves, for which the new facility for the creation of drawing rights cannot, under the rules adopted, provide replacement. This threat to international monetary stability must not be allowed to continue; international arrangements to avert the switches between reserve assets or to replace unwanted currency reserves with other reserve assets are urgently needed.

All four problems can be formulated in terms of "monetary reserves." The liquidity problem refers to the failure to achieve an adequate gradual *increase* in the total of reserves. The confidence problem refers to possible demands for changes in the *composition* of reserves and to the threatening *destruction* of reserves in the course of such changes. The adjustment problem refers to the failure of the system to stop or reverse changes in the international *distribution* of reserves arising from persistent deficits and surpluses in the payments positions of particular countries. The problem of involuntary development aid refers to the failure of some developing countries to hold on to funds allocated to them for reserve purposes and to resist the temptation of using them for meeting shortages of *long-term capital*.

The plan agreed upon in Rio de Janeiro may, if executed wisely, solve the liquidity problem. The problem of involuntary development aid is not serious. But the problems of adjustment and of confidence are still unsolved and require urgent attention. I shall return to them in Part 6.

5.

Semantic and Theoretic Explanations

It remains to make good on a promise given in the second part of this essay. When it was found that some of the governments agreeing on the new arrangements were disagreeing on the interpretation of their meaning, I promised to explore the semantic and theoretic differences that account for the divergent judgments.

If semantic fog is dispelled and clearer vision is thereby afforded, some apprehension and uneasiness may disappear. Possibly, however, mere apprehension may give way to genuine opposition: unwonted clarity of thought and language may expose hitherto concealed issues of substantive disagreement — and this may endanger ratification of the agreement. I prefer to think that, in the long run, clear vision is conducive to progress, even though steps taken under conditions of limited visibility may be in the right direction.

Drawing Rights and Reserve Units

The fundamental concepts and word meanings on which clarity has to be sought are those of money and credit. But certain much narrower, more technical terms have also lately, indeed within a few months, changed their meanings, and this semantic instability may be responsible for misunderstandings.

The Report of the Deputies of the Group of Ten, submitted to the Ministers and Governors in July 1966, distinguished two alternative approaches to the creation of new reserve assets: "The two basic forms of reserve asset that we have considered are drawing rights and reserve units."[1] The chief difference was that drawing rights were seen as rights against the Fund, to draw convertible currencies from the IMF (or another agency), whereas reserve units were claims transferable directly among participants. When use limits and holding limits were discussed, a comment was added to the effect that the discussion of these techniques "concerns mainly schemes which are based on units and not on drawing rights."[2]

However, "although drawing rights and reserve units have distinctive attributes, . . . it was recognized that at the margin their characteristics tend to merge. If drawing rights were made directly transferable . . . they would be rather similar to units. And units that involved guided transferability by an agent would be rather close to drawing rights. Nevertheless most members see significant differences in the manner of transferring reserve units and drawing rights and especially in the attitudes of monetary authorities and of the general public toward the two types of assets."[3]

Evidently, the quick change in the word meanings was a matter of diplomatic convenience. The term "reserve unit" had become unacceptable to one government. By calling the new reserve asset "drawing right," although it was no longer a right to draw currencies from the Fund and although it was made directly transferable among participants, it became possible to agree on its creation. If this terminological flexibility is understood, there should be no difficulty in comprehending the character of the special drawing rights adopted by the Rio Agreement.

This is not to say that the reserve asset outlined by the Rio Agreement would be more appropriately called a "reserve unit." For, what in 1966 was discussed under this designation was also conceived as a claim against the Fund or some similar central debtor, either in the form of a "deposit" or as an "overdraft facility."[4] What

---

[1] Emminger Report, *op. cit.*, § 52.

[2] *Ibid.*, § 71.

[3] *Ibid.*, § 52.

[4] *Ibid.*, § 54.

the Outline actually creates is neither a drawing right nor a reserve unit in the meanings of the 1966 Report. Is it credit? Is it money?

Credit: A Semantic Mess

"We consent to a possible mechanism for new credits, accompanied by a reform of the IMF, and nothing more." If M. Debré, who made this statement in Rio, regards SDR's as nothing but credit, and the agreed arrangements as merely an improved "method of granting international credit," it would be most unwise to try to prove him wrong. But, even quite apart from diplomatic considerations, he could not be proved wrong, because among the many meanings of "credit" there are several that can make his propositions perfectly true. Indeed, we could, if we thought it worth while, compose mutually contradictory statements about credit and demonstrate each to be true under some of the accepted meanings of the word.

The Oxford Dictionary gives twelve meanings of the noun "credit," Webster's also gives twelve. I can do even better, but will merely list some of the synonyms of credit in the different meanings of the word. Confidence, trust, deferred payment, loan, borrowing, loanable funds, loan-and-securities portfolio, deposit liabilities, bank money, entry in customer's favor, balance in customer's favor, offsets to debits; all these relate to commercial or financial operations.[5] In

---

[5] It may be helpful to some if I formulate sentences containing "credit" in each of these meanings:

(1) "All money depends on *credit*" — in the sense (a) that we accept it only because we have *confidence* in others accepting it from us in exchange for things we want, and (b) that we hold it only because we have *confidence* that its exchange value will not vanish at too rapid a rate.

(2) "Lending, in most instances, depends on *credit*" — in the sense that the lender *trusts* the borrower's probity and ability to repay.

(3) "In several industries all suppliers are prepared to sell on *credit*" — in the sense that they are willing to *defer payment for* the goods sold.

(4) "The bank offered me a *credit* of a million dollars" — meaning that I was offered a *loan* in the amount stated.

(footnote continued on the following page)

addition, there are also some more general meanings of credit: belief, commendation, attribution, asset, repute.[6]

Practically anything financial has something to do with money and, hence, with confidence in its acceptability and its exchange

---

(footnote 5 continued from previous page)

(5) "I neither need nor want *credit*" — meaning that I neither need nor want to *borrow*.

(6) "The *credit* market shows signs of increased tightness" — meaning that an excess demand for *loanable funds* has raised interest rates.

(7) "The Federal Reserve Banks report that *credit* outstanding has increased by x per cent over the last six months" — meaning that their *portfolio of securities and loans* has increased at the rate mentioned.

(8) "A reduction of reserve requirements will allow a creation of *credit* by the member banks" — meaning that the *deposit liabilities* of the banks may be increased as a result of increased loans and purchases of securities by the member banks.

(9) "Effective demand reflects the substantial *credit* creation of the last year" — meaning that creation of *bank money* has resulted in increased demand for goods and services.

(10) "The proceeds from the foreign exchange sold to the bank were entered as a *credit* on the customer's account" — meaning that an *entry* was made on the side showing the customer's claims against the bank.

(11) "His account shows a net *credit* of $100,000" — meaning that his deposit account in the bank shows this amount as a *balance in his favor*.

(12) "Capital and surplus are shown on the *credit* side of the balance sheet" — meaning that the total of assets, shown on the debit side, is offset by the total of *liabilities and the equity* of the owners of the business.

Differences in the meanings of a word can be shown most clearly by translation into foreign languages. The German equivalents of "credit" in the twelve sentences are (1) and (2) *Vertrauen*, (3) *Zahlungsfrist*, (4) *Darlehen*, (5) *Ausborgen*, (6) *Leihkapital*, (7) *Inlandsaktiva (Wertpapiere und Wechsel)*, (8) *Sichtverbindlichkeiten*, (9) *Bankgeld*, (10) *Gutschrift*, (11) *Guthaben*, (12) *Habenseite*.

[6] Again, sentences containing "credit" in these meanings shall be proposed:

(13) "We may give full *credit* to the report that M. Debré favored an average net use of SDR's of only 50 per cent of the cumulative allocations" — meaning that *belief* in the report seems justified.

(14) "It does him *credit* that he did not insist on this low limit" — meaning that he deserves *commendation*.

(15) "Much of the *credit* for reaching a compromise is due to Dr. Emminger" — meaning that we may attribute the success largely to him.

(16) "Mr. Schweitzer is a *credit* to his native country" — meaning that he is an *asset* to the French nation, that he adds to its *repute*.

value. This first meaning of credit allows us to link any scheme, arrangement, or institution concerning monetary or financial affairs with credit. Since the newly instituted special drawing rights will be accepted by participating central banks in exchange for convertible currencies, these banks must have confidence in their being accepted also by the other participants; and since they will be held by central banks, not just for brief intervals but for long periods and to some extent forever, these banks must have confidence in the maintenance of their exchange value. Thus, the scheme is based on *credit* in the sense of confidence.

The three bookkeeping meanings of credit will also be involved in the new scheme. There will be entries and balances in accounts and items in balance sheets. A participant receiving SDR's as an original allocation or as transfer will receive a credit on the account of the Special Drawing Account; and for allocated amounts the participant will credit a "contingent liabilities" account (or some item of the sort). Since SDR's will "exist" only when they are recorded on the books of the Special Drawing Account of the IMF, one may even say that they *are* credit in the sense of entries and balances on the participants' accounts.

One cannot know whether or not these are the associations in the minds of those who stress that the new facility is a mechanism for new credits "and nothing more." A few other interpretations are also possible. One may recall, for example, the old textbook distinction between commodity money and credit money. According to this classification, any money that is not also a commodity (and hence cannot be used for purposes other than as a means of exchange and a store of value) is, by definition, *credit money*. Applied to international money, or international reserve assets, the same distinction differentiates gold reserves and credit reserves; SDR's are in the second category. (I prefer, however, to call them "fiduciary reserves.")

Two other connections between credit and the new international monetary facility can be shown to be relevant. One relates to the "credit" which a surplus country grants to deficit countries as it gives up real resources in exchange for claims against foreign resources to be used at some indefinite time in the future. (I shall defer the discussion of this issue until later in this chapter.) The other is the causal connection between credit extension and money supply.[7] This is not a matter of semantics but of economic theory, and it must be understood clearly before one can hope to grasp some of the official and unofficial interpretations of the new scheme.

Credit Extension and Money Supply

The extension of credit may increase or leave unchanged the total amount of money held by the community. In this sentence, "credit" is used in the sense of a new loan being granted to a borrower, and "money" in the sense of means of exchange and payment.

A new loan will leave the stock of money unchanged if the lender parts with money he has held and the borrower receives what the lender parts with; as the borrower then uses the borrowed money to make payments to others, these others will receive what the borrower, and before him the lender, has parted with. Thus, credit has been extended but the stock of money has not increased.

A new loan will increase the stock of money if the lender's obligations are accepted as money by the borrower and his payees, so that the lender does not have to reduce his holdings of money, but increases his liabilities instead. Lenders whose liabilities are money to those who hold them are called banks. The statement made will hold also, or especially, for the whole group of banks, for even if some of these lenders have to give up some of their money assets in the process, these money assets may accrue to other banks with the result that the money assets of all banks together are unchanged and a net increase in their sight liabilities — money to the holders — offsets the increase in their loan portfolio.

Credit, in one of the meanings, comprises a bank's security holdings in addition to its portfolio of short-term loans. Accordingly, credit expansion may include, besides new loans, additional purchases of securities. Short-term lending is often seen as purchase

---

[7] This was probably the intended reference when Professor Schiller, the German Minister for Economic Affairs, in his statement at Rio, said that "as in the national field, money is created by credit."

of promises to pay (promissory notes, bills of exchange), and "credit outstanding" measured by the entire portfolio of domestic credit instruments acquired: investments in securities as well as short-term loans. A significant difference between credit expansion through loans and credit expansion through purchases of securities is that the latter is a unilateral decision of the bank while the former presupposes the borrowers' demand for loans.

One may generalize that the extension of bank loans leads to an increase in the money supply as, if, and when the expansion of the portfolio of the banks is not offset by a decline in other bank assets but rather by increases in the banks' liquid liabilities.

Analogous propositions can be formulated on the level of international credit and the creation of international reserves. Thus, an international agency whose liquid liabilities and promises to pay are regarded as monetary reserves by national monetary authorities can create international reserves by making loans and/or purchasing securities. As its portfolio of loans and securities increases, its liquid liabilities — and therefore the international reserve assets held by the national authorities — increase *pari passu*.

Now that it is understood that the extension of loans may create money — national money if the lenders are domestic banks, international money (reserves) if they are international institutions — it should also be clear that (a) not every extension of loans creates money and (b) not all money is created by extension of loans. I suspect that some of the divergences in the interpretation of the scheme to create and allocate special drawing rights are due to rash or incomplete analyses of the relationships in question. Some who recognize that new reserve assets are created under the new scheme jump to the conclusion that it must involve an extension of loans. Others who incline to disregard or de-emphasize the creation of reserve assets under the scheme, but recognize that it enables countries to spend money that they have not earned, conclude that only an extension of loans can accomplish such a feat.

In fact, however, the scheme does not include the extension of any loans nor the increase of a loans-and-securities portfolio by any lender or investor. The Special Drawing Account of the IMF will allocate SDR's to all participants, but not on a borrower's application nor on a decision to invest in securities (or currencies). The SDR's come into existence as they are allocated, but not in the process of any lending or investment by the Fund or anybody else. If one regards the SDR's as international money (accepted and held by national monetary authorities and used for purchases of convertible currencies from one another), then one must take the scheme as one of *money creation without credit extension*.

In the course of the discussions and negotiations leading to the Rio Agreement a large variety of plans had been proposed and examined, some of which involved reserve creation through credit extension, others credit extension without reserve creation, and still others credit extension with only temporary increases in reserves. It is easy to overlook subtle differences among the alternative schemes and to think that what is true for one holds also for another.

Permanent and Impermanent Reserves

The largest number of alternative schemes, examined but not adopted by the negotiating parties, involved reserve creation through credit expansion — credit in the sense of the loans-and-securities portfolio of an international agency. A few of these schemes would produce only temporary increases in reserves, but most of them would create permanent reserve assets.

Increases in reserves are likely to be *temporary* if they result from loans extended by an international agency to national monetary authorities who want to borrow; they are *semi-permanent* if they result from purchases of securities at the discretion of the international agency; they are *permanent* if they result from the acquisition of dormant, nonmaturing liabilities of participating countries which are not supposed to redeem or repurchase them as long as the scheme is in operation.[8]

---

[8] This discussion of the permanence of reserves created under alternative schemes may raise the question of the permanence of the reserves existing

(footnote continued on the following page)

In all three of these cases the international agency acquires additional assets and thereby increases its liabilities (which are held as monetary reserves by national monetary authorities). These liabilities disappear again when the assets are disposed of (redeemed, sold, or otherwise liquidated). If the assets are loans, they are canceled when the loans are repaid. If the assets are securities, they are unloaded when the agency so decides. If the assets are dormant, nonmaturing liabilities of the participating countries, they remain on the books of the agency for good.

The first of the three types is the scheme most appropriately called a "credit facility." It is a facility for would-be borrowers to obtain loans which they expect and are expected to repay as soon as possible. Such a scheme increases monetary reserves only temporarily. If Country A is in payments deficit and short of reserves,

---

(footnote 8 continued from previous page)

now. The least permanent of the existing reserve assets are the claims that have arisen under bilateral or multilateral lending arrangements among monetary authorities. These claims are generated by short-term lending under swap agreements, by the acquisition of bonds of short maturity, and by loans under the General Arrangement to Borrow.

Holdings of foreign exchange are reserves held at the holder's pleasure or convenience. As long as no "life insurance" is arranged for official holdings of dollars and pounds, some of these reserves can disappear much faster than we care to visualize. Massive conversions into gold would either "liquidate" — eliminate — much of the existing liquidity or "illiquidate" — freeze — what are now regarded as liquid reserve assets (and thereby reduce their reserve quality).

Monetary gold is permanent as long as the gold remains monetary. Until three years ago, the permanence of gold reserves in the system as a whole was not in question. Now that private demand for gold exceeds private supply, losses of official holdings are no longer hypothetical; such losses have occurred for three years and may become an annual recurrence. One need not expect, however, that these reductions of gold reserves will take on massive dimensions in the next few years.

IMF reserve positions are not permanent either. For example, when a country replenishes its partly depleted credit tranche by repurchasing its own currency with a convertible currency, the country whose currency is paid into the Fund will find its super-gold-tranche position reduced. Or, when a country draws down its gold-tranche position by purchasing the currency of a country that, through its past drawings, has gone well into its credit tranche, there will be a net reduction in IMF reserve positions. Total IMF reserve positions do not fluctuate very widely, but they can decrease as well as increase.

it applies for a loan from the international agency. Receiving the loan, it can finance its deficit. Country B, running a surplus, receives payment from Country A in the form of a deposit liability of the international agency. If the adjustment processes work properly, Country A will in due course have a payments surplus, and Country B a deficit. Country B can now use the reserves it previously received; it uses them to pay Country A; and the latter can pay its debt to the international agency. As the loan is repaid, both the assets and liabilities of the agency are reduced. The increase in monetary reserves, brought about by the loan, is canceled as the loan is repaid. International credit facilities are therefore unsuitable as mechanisms to provide regular increases in international reserves. Only when new borrowings exceed repayments, will total monetary reserves increase; they will decline when new borrowings are smaller than repayments.

The second type is credit creation in the wider sense of the word, including in total "credit outstanding" the open-market purchases of securities. Most countries have opposed schemes of this sort because they do not want to entrust an international agency with discretionary power to buy and sell selected securities in the capital markets of the various nations.

The third type is the only technique of creating permanent monetary reserves by way of credit extension. It differs in two essential respects from credit facilities that are available on request: (1) the countries' liabilities that are to be held as (dormant) assets by the international agency are not acquired when countries need funds, or want funds, but rather at stated, predetermined points of time; (2) the liabilities of the countries are not repaid, neither sooner nor later; they stay alive, though dormant, so that the liquid liabilities of the international agency which they bring into being can also stay alive and active.

None of the three types, let it be repeated, was adopted. The scheme that was adopted comes closest to the third of the rejected types, in that it too provides for the creation of permanent reserve assets; but it differs from the third type in that there will be no international agency that acquires liabilities from national authorities and incurs liabilities to them. The Special Drawing Account will extend no loans and contract no debts. It will follow Polonius' advice: "neither a borrower, nor a lender be."

The Difference
between Reconstitution and Repayment

The official French position, that "the plan provides for the possible extending of credit facilities," emphasizes the conception of "repayment." Although "provision has been made for generous terms and conditions of repayment," M. Debré stated at Rio, "rules of repayment nevertheless exist" and are quite "categorical." The reference is to the requirement of reconstitution of minimum balances. Under these provisions, "a country that drew its entire allocation at the beginning of the operation of the system would be obliged to repay it in full at the end of a three-and-a-half-year period, and would be unable to make any further drawing until the end of the fifth year." The German interpretation appears to support this point of view inasmuch as Dr. Schiller, in his statement at Rio, characterized "the new mechanism" as being "based on the principles of credit and repayability."

It is fair to try to understand how one may see in the reconstitution of a positive balance the same process as in the repayment of a debt. This is quite easy if one thinks of the actions and policies of an individual client: whether he wants to repay a debt or to build up a positive cash balance, in both cases he will have to reduce his spending relative to his receipts. The same change in his payments position will enable him to improve his cash position or to reduce his debts. This holds for a whole country no less than for an individual household or an individual business firm.

There are, of course, differences between the two objectives even from the point of view of individual decision-makers — national authorities, commercial-bank managers, other corporate executives, and households. The propensity to spend, or to induce spending, may be different if the spending means running up debts rather than running down cash balances. The psychological differences may prevail even if the time within which debts have to be paid is as long as the time within which balances have to be replenished. But the really important difference between reconstituting balances and repaying loans becomes relevant on the level of the system as a whole.

The important difference lies in the permanence or impermanence of the total stock of money or, with regard to the international system, the total stock of reserve assets. In systems in which national moneys or international reserve assets are created by the extension of repayable loans, these money assets are destroyed by the repayment of the loans. The payments of debts to a money-creating institution cancels some of the debt-money that had been issued. This is altogether different in the case of the special drawing rights to be created and allocated under the new system. If individual countries, having used large parts of their SDR's, reconstitute their balances, SDR's are transferred but not destroyed. Just as *use* of SDR's neither increases nor reduces the total of SDR's in the possession of the participating countries, *reconstitution* of balances by those who, under the rules, are obliged to replenish their holdings, will leave the total unchanged.

This difference between the two otherwise "analogous" processes is so categorical that one can understand why most of the interpreters of the Outline do not speak of repayment when they refer to the rules for reconstitution of balances.

Money Not Spent versus Credit Not Used

Yet another possible divergence in monetary theory may underlie the differences in the interpretation of the new system. It goes back to an old controversy regarding the relative importance of the quantity and the utilization of money, that is, of the demand for money to hold and the actual spending of money. On an international level, the analogous question relates to the relative importance of the *stock* of official monetary reserves and of the current *use* of reserves in the financing of payments deficits.

If one holds that neither the size nor changes in the size of total reserves really matter, if what counts is only the use that is made of reserves in deficit situations, then it may actually not be essential whether deficits are financed out of existing reserves or rather out of new borrowings, creating new reserves *ad hoc*. Borrowing and spending would be equivalent; nonspending and nonborrowing would be equivalent too.

This equivalence is, as a matter of fact, quite apropos as far as the transfer of real resources is concerned. A payments deficit, whether financed out of existing monetary reserves or out of new borrowing from an international or foreign institution, reflects a draft on the resources of foreign countries. Deficit countries receive goods and services (or perhaps titles to investment) from surplus countries. In exchange for these resources the latter accept some money assets which they can use to buy foreign resources some time in the future, when their payments surpluses have turned into payments deficits. This notion, the exchange of present resources for future resources, may bulk large in the minds of those who insist on calling any financing of payments balances a "credit" from surplus to deficit countries. In this case, of course, the acceptance of gold by a surplus country is also "credit," indeed, not one bit less so than the acceptance of pieces of paper or of ink entries on a bookkeeper's account.

When the focus is on the net transfer of real resources among countries, the only really significant distinction is whether the real transfer represents a gift or a capital movement. Gifts may be explicit or concealed. They are sometimes disguised in the form of non-interest-bearing loans that will eventually be forgiven or defaulted (so-called fuzzy loans). They are sometimes concealed, even from the donor country itself, if the country accumulates monetary gold stocks on which it collects no interest and which it will never use in payment for later deficits. In this case, the "credit" to countries in deficit is never repaid in real resources, and the gold, received as a token entitling to pay for a future payments deficit, remains stored and forever unused. On the other hand, a genuine credit to deficit countries usually provides for a return flow of interest and principal. The statistician will record the credit either as a capital outflow from the surplus country (if securities are acquired from, or loans granted to, foreigners) or as an increase in monetary reserves (if foreign balances, short-term securities, or international money assets are acquired by the monetary authorities). In this conception, every current surplus that is expected sooner or later to be turned into a current deficit is "credit" granted to the rest of the world — regardless of whether the surplus country accepts securities, gold, liquid balances, or drawing rights as evidences of its claim against the real resources of the world. From this point of view it is immaterial whether deficit countries have had reserves to finance their deficits or were able to make use of "credit facilities."

May one reasonably infer from these statements that it makes no difference whether SDR's are allocated to all participants in predetermined amounts or special loans are extended to countries in deficit? A country not in deficit would not make use of its allocated SDR's, just as it would not apply for a loan. Is there no difference between money not spent and credit not used? To think so is to forget that payments balances depend on the policies of the countries concerned and that policies depend to a significant degree on reserve positions and, especially, on changes in reserve positions. I have discussed these relationships earlier in this essay, epecially when I examined the liberalizing, inflationary, and resource-transferring impacts and influences of the allocation of SDR's. To assume that SDR allocations and loans to finance payments deficits are "equivalent" in all respects is to assume either that deficits are independent of policies or that policies are not affected by changes in payments and reserve positions. These assumptions are contrary to experience.

Credit or No Credit?

After all this filling and backing on the credit character of SDR's, the reader may well be more confused than ever. Are the SDR's credit or are they not? Of course they are, and they are not, depending on the sense intended. It may be helpful to have a summary of this discussion in the form of sets of legitimate and illegitimate statements. I begin with legitimate ones.

1. SDR's will be reserve assets held by monetary authorities. Like most money assets, but unlike gold, they will not be traded in commodity markets and cannot be used for filling teeth or coating parts of electronic instruments. Thus, they will not be commodity reserves, but fiduciary or *credit reserves*.

2. SDR's, like all other money assets, will be based on *credit in the sense of confidence* (a) in their being accepted by others — in this case, by other monetary authorities — and (b) in their not losing their exchange value any faster than their chief substitutes, that is, gold and reserve currencies.

3. SDR's will be created and allocated by *credit entries* being made in the country accounts kept by the Special Drawing Account of the Fund.

4. SDR's will be *credit balances* of the participating countries in the accounting records kept by the Special Drawing Account.

5. SDR's, both those received as allocations and those received as transfers from other countries, will be treated as assets on the debit side of the balance sheets of the monetary authorities. The receipt of allocated SDR's will require an offsetting item on the *credit side* of the balance sheet, probably under the designation of contingent liabilities for the case of withdrawal or liquidation.

6. SDR's will be used by countries to finance some of their deficits and will be accepted by countries in payments surplus. Inasmuch as such surpluses imply giving up real resources in exchange for money assets which represent claims on foreign resources for eventual use in the future, surpluses financed by the acceptance of SDR's — as of any other money assets — can be characterized as *credits*, or loans of real resources, to deficit countries.

Now a few wrong statements, with reasons why we find them wrong.

A. SDR's will be created by extensions of *credit by the Fund.* Wrong; no credits, or loans, will be extended by the Special Drawing Account of the Fund.

B. SDR's will be created by extension of *credit by the countries participating* in the scheme and undertaking the obligation to honor the drawing rights when presented. Wrong; an obligation to accept a money asset in payment constitutes neither a loan nor a promise to lend.

C. SDR's will be transferred by deficit countries to countries in strong reserve positions against surrender of convertible currencies by the latter, a transaction that will constitute[9] *credit extended by the recipient* of the SDR's to the user of SDR's. Wrong; the acceptance of SDR's does not create a claim against the user of the SDR's, just as the acceptance of money by a seller of goods does not create a claim against the buyer who has used money in payment for his purchase.

D.   SDR's cannot be used without limit; a country having used its allocated SDR's beyond the stated limit will be compelled to reconstitute its holdings of SDR's, which is the same as the *repayment of a credit*. Wrong; while there are close similarities in the behavior prerequisite to debt payment and behavior prerequisite to building up a cash position, repaying loans and accumulating cash are different things and have different consequences for the system as a whole.

Money or No Money?

Just as it has been possible to conclude that SDR's are and are not credit, depending on what meaning is given to the word, one may state that SDR's are money and are not money. It all depends on what is meant by the word "money."

There is hardly a textbook on money that fails to distinguish the three "main functions" of money — to be medium of exchange (means of payment); store of value; and unit of account (standard of value). The better textbooks go on to discuss the dilemma faced when a particular currency serves only one or two of these functions. The best textbooks conclude that only the first of the three functions should be taken as the criterion in the definition, with the other two being regarded only as usual but not necessary attributes. (For example, in the period of hyper-inflation the German mark still was means of payment but had stopped being used either as store of value or as unit of account.)

However, even after one agrees on this definition of money,

---

[9]The difference between propositions B and C is in the timing of the alleged extension of credit. Statement B specifies as credit extension the undertaking of the obligation to accept SDR's, Statement C the actual acceptance of SDR's transferred by a participating country.

there remain the questions of when? to whom? and for what? Even at the same time, payments are made with different "moneys" among different people, in different circles, and for different kinds of transactions. For example, payments for securities transactions by clients of stockbrokers are made chiefly by means of credit balances with their brokers; payments for goods and services among individuals and corporations within the United States are made chiefly by means of check deposits in commercial banks; payments of clearing balances among banks in the United States are made in "federal funds," that is, with deposit claims on Federal Reserve Banks; payments among the twelve Federal Reserve Banks are made in gold certificates of the United States Treasury; payments in the largest markets for gold abroad are made chiefly in bank checks in United States dollars; likewise, most payments for national currencies in the largest foreign-exchange markets are made in United States dollars.

Accepting, then, the notion that money for a certain group need not be money for another, one may say that SDR's are money for the participants in the Special Drawing Account. Each participant can buy convertible currency from other participants and pay for it with SDR's. The SDR's are, therefore, means of payment for convertible currencies acquired by one national monetary authority from another.

On the other hand, if somebody insisted that money had to be defined as means of payment for ordinary people buying such things as peanuts and ice-cream cones; or if someone were to insist — rather foolishly, in my opinion — that money was essentially a unit of account (standard of value) and that nothing except a unit of account was money, then, obviously, SDR's would not be money. Gold, in this case, would not be money either, for it is neither a means of payment nor a unit of account.

Quibbles about Words:
Sometimes Useless, Sometimes Important

Many people are contemptuous of debates about semantics. To be sure, quibbles about words are often useless, perhaps more often than not. There is a pragmatic test for deciding whether it is useless, helpful, or even imperative to agree on word meanings: one asks what difference it would make if the semantic quarrel were decided one way or the other.

Take, for example, the question, often discussed in the United States, whether time deposits in commercial banks are or are not money. The answer would make no difference to depositors, and no difference to bankers. But it would make a difference to central-bank managers and to economic analysts. While commercial bankers may call the question useless, central-bank managers ought to understand that the answer may be important for decisions on monetary policy; and economists must decide the question for their analyses of trends and cyclical changes in financial conditions.

Another example may reinforce our conclusion. If a country operates a combined postal money-order and postal savings system which people generally use in the same fashion as the Americans and British use commercial-bank checks, this postal payments system will "work" no matter whether the balances in the postal accounts are called money, credit, deposits, or what not. The precise meanings of these words, important as they may be for some purposes, are irrelevant for the functioning of the system and uninteresting to its managers as well as to its clients. The significance of the semantic decision lies in the understanding of certain economic relationships — of concern only to economists, government officials, and legislators.[10]

The disagreements about the "true character" of SDR's appear as useless quibbles to some, but as important problems to others. If the Rio Agreement is ratified by the member countries of the Fund and if the facility thus established is put into operation, it does not

---

[10] Analogous examples can be given from all fields. Here is one from physics: a certain apparatus may be widely used and may work satisfactorily even though its users do not know — and those who think they know do not agree — whether the essential processes in its operation are magnetic, electric, electronic, atomic, nuclear, etc. The differences in question are not "philosophic," and a physicist may be shocked by the layman's ignorance regarding these designations. But for all practical purposes the apparatus will work regardless of the confusion in the minds and in the talk of its actual users.

matter whether the Ministers and Governors think of the allocation of SDR's as extension of credit, as creation and distribution of money, or as any other financial hocus-pocus. The system can work to the satisfaction of anyone concerned even if the disagreement on the economic character and economic function of the SDR's continues. The chief architects of the system knew what they were doing.

6.

Unfinished Business

Two or three times in this essay I have warned that the agenda for negotiations on international monetary problems includes an item "unfinished business" that promises or threatens to be more demanding than anything accomplished thus far. The most urgent problems are those of adjustment to restore balance in international payments and of confidence to avoid destruction of existing currency reserves. Both these problems are closely connected with the gnawing question of gold.

I shall first present brief descriptions of the apparently intractable problems: the persistent imbalance of payments of the United States, the precarious "overhang" of dollars in private and official possession abroad, and the massive speculation in gold. I shall then proceed to a discussion of the alternatives that actually or seemingly offer themselves for dealing with what will clearly manifest itself as a frightful predicament.

The Payments Deficit of the United States

The United States has been running a deficit in its balance of payments since 1950, that is, for 18 years, except in 1957, the year following the Suez crisis. (Even for that year a deficit would be shown if "errors and omissions," carrying a positive sign at the time, were not included as receipts.) The computation of a deficit is, of course, a matter of statistical convention, and by the conventions of the 1950's one would still be speaking of American "surpluses," as was done when additional dollar balances were in heavy demand by almost all foreign nations. But by the definitions now most widely adopted,[1] the United States ran deficits in the 1950's as well as in the 1960's. The hard fact behind all statistical calculations is that the United States, between 1949 and 1967, has seen its monetary gold

---

[1] See footnote on the following page.

stock decline from $24.6 billion to $12 billion and its liquid liabilities to foreign monetary authorities increase from $3.2 billion to $15 billion. (By the middle of March 1968 the gold reserves were down to $10.5 billion and the official liabilities were up to nearly $16 billion.)

No one was worried about these deficits between 1950 and 1958. Indeed, most commentators were pleased about the redistribution of gold and about the increase in dollar reserves of the non-dollar countries during these years of "dollar shortage." Later, however, the appetite for official dollar reserves had been fully satisfied and misgivings about a "dollar glut," a supply of more dollars than were wanted, began to be voiced. As a matter of fact, the supply of dollars increased, instead of declining, and many of the unwanted dollars were returned to the United States for conversion into gold. From December 1957 to December 1961, the monetary gold stock of the United States fell from $22.9 billion to $16.9 billion.

Beginning in 1960 the United States adopted a series of measures designed to reduce or remove the payments deficit. These measures were of two kinds: (1) selective correctives, that is, measures supposed to operate on particular types of transactions and to improve selected items in the balance of payments, and (2) general adjustment policies, that is, policies to affect the general level of incomes and prices in ways that would through market forces improve the balance on goods and services.

The adjustment process seemed to work satisfactorily for a number of years, thanks chiefly to the fact that price levels were kept relatively stable in the United States but rose substantially in many other countries, especially in the large industrial countries of Europe. This allowed the American export balance of goods and services to increase from $2.2 billion in 1958 to $8.5 billion in 1964. However, a sharp increase in capital outflows canceled out much of the

---

(footnote referred to on page 96.)

[1] At present the United States calculates two official figures: the deficit on the "liquidity basis," and the deficit on the "official-settlements basis." Two other significant concepts are the deficit in the "basic balance" and the decline in "net foreign reserves." Although these four balances are drastically different, the deficit has persisted no matter which of the four concepts is used.

improvement of the current account: from 1959 to 1965 the outflow of private long-term capital increased from $1.6 billion to $4.4 billion. (One must not assume, however, that these changes are independent of one another; it is quite likely that the increase in capital outflow stimulated foreign demand and thus helped increase commodity exports from the United States.)

After 1964, the adjustment process came to a halt, probably because of an updrift of incomes and prices in the United States and a simultaneous attenuation of wage-and-price inflations in Europe.[2] The American export balance of goods and services began to decline: from the $8.5 billion in 1964 it fell to $5.1 billion in 1966.

To record that the adjustment process came to a halt is not to say that adjustment policies will not work. They will, if consistently pursued. Nor is it to condemn the United States for not pursuing them consistently. The government evidently believed that policies of restraining the increase in effective demand were too costly in terms of employment and national product. It was a conscious decision to give prime consideration to the objective of achieving greater employment through stepping up aggregate demand. An economist may have his own value judgments about which ought to be more important to the nation: more employment or a smaller payments deficit. But the decisions are made by governments.[3] In any case, the expansion of aggregate demand in the

---

[2] Wholesale prices in the United States, which had been virtually unchanged for six years — from 1958 to 1964 — rose from March 1965 to August 1966 at an annual rate of 3.8 per cent.

[3] The economist should not be silent, however, when faulty arguments are presented by the government. When a reduction of income taxes was proposed by the government and legislated by the Congress in 1964, economists outside Washington expected that the resulting increase in domestic consumption and investment would increase imports and reduce the export surplus. Yet, President Johnson, in his *Economic Report* of January 1964, predicted that

> With the tax cut, our *balance of payments* will benefit from basic improvements — in our ability to compete in world markets as costs are cut directly through lower taxes and indirectly through modernization; — and in our ability to retain and attract capital as returns on domestic investment rise with higher volume and lower unit costs [p. 9].

This argument was specious, to put it mildly.

United States halted and reversed the improvement in the current balance and did not prevent a drastic deterioration of the capital balance.

The corrective measures, recommended by those who believe that you can correct a deficit by picking particular items in the balance of payments and working on them by means of selective restrictions and controls, have had only the success expected by (allegedly "unrealistic") economic theorists: if a chosen item was improved and the dollar outflow reduced under that particular heading, trouble quickly arose for another item, leaving the over-all payments deficit just about where it was. More will be said later on the question of "item-picking" and on the effectiveness of selective controls. One point, however, calls for reflection now. The deficit in the balance of payments has been between one and four billion dollars during the past 18 years. With a gross national product of over $800 billion at the end of 1967, and between $500 and $750 billion in the past seven years, why should it be so difficult to improve the balance of goods and services by just another two billion dollars? With all controls and restraints, the payments deficit has refused to budge and the balance of international transactions has not done us the favor of improving by as little as one-half of 1 per cent of the gross national product. This, I believe, is most impressive. It impresses me chiefly as an indication of the great strength of market forces and an indication of the humbling weakness of governmental controls.

The upshot of it all is that after 18 years the payments deficit of the United States is worse than ever and shows no signs of improvement.

In the past, the deficits have been financed partly by increases in liquid liabilities to foreign holders of dollars and partly by drains on the monetary gold stock. It now looks as if in the future our deficits may have to be financed increasingly, and perhaps mainly, by the surrender of gold. If so, the United States will have spent all its gold within four or five years — provided it has not surrendered it even earlier through conversions of dollars which foreign holders have accumulated in previous years.

The Dollar Overhang from Earlier Years

On September 30, 1967, the national monetary authorities of the noncommunist countries held a total of 14.4 billion of United States dollars; private foreign holdings of dollars totaled 15.1 billion. The combined total of $29.5 billion,[4] had been accumulated chiefly in the years between 1950 and 1965.

The division of foreign dollar holdings into official and private is significant on several grounds, although it is well known that central banks on occasion "place" some of their dollar holdings with commercial banks.[5] As a consequence, published figures do not tell the complete story in that they do not reveal how many private holdings are actually hidden monetary reserves of the central bank. But to the extent that the statistics tell the correct story, the division is important, especially because of the different motives for holding dollars.

Private foreign dollar balances are held almost entirely for transactions purposes. The "transactions demand" for dollar balances on the part of commercial banks and traders abroad is determined by daily, weekly, monthly, and seasonal variations in receipts and expenditures, by interest-rate differentials, by the cost of foreign-exchange operations, and by expected changes in exchange rates. Official dollar holdings, on the other hand, are determined largely by political considerations. The central banker of a large industrial country does not look in the first place at the alternative costs and earnings of his asset-mix, but rather on the advantages or necessities of international financial cooperation or noncooperation. These differences in motivation bear on the problem of the large liquid liabilities of the United States to foreign

---

[4] Total liquid dollar liabilities were $31.2 billion, if the debts to the International Monetary Fund ($1.0 billion) and to other international organizations ($0.7 billion) are included.

[5] The central bank does this by way of swap or repurchase agreements that make it attractive for commercial banks to use their excess reserves for acquiring the dollar assets, which yield interest and a small gain in the resale price. The main purpose of the central bank is to syphon off some excessive lending capacity, or excess liquidity, of the banking system; in this fashion dollar assets take the place of government securities in open-market operations.

holders and of the danger that these dollar holdings may be drastically reduced.

Not all "asset switching" has the same effects. If there is a massive flight into gold, it need not be a flight from the dollar; and if there is a massive flight from the dollar, it need not be into gold. Private foreign holders of dollars who wish to get rid of their dollars may prefer to hold other currencies which they regard as safer. And foreign hoarders or speculators who wish to buy gold may intend to reduce their holdings, not of dollars, but of other currencies, especially their own. To equate an increase in the demand for gold hoards with a decrease in the demand for dollar balances may therefore be wrong. Of the non-dollar-holder's flight into gold I shall talk later; let us first concentrate on the danger of a flight from the dollar, either into gold or into other currencies.

The decision of a private foreign holder of dollars to exchange them into gold can be regarded as exceptional. Ordinarily, he needs his working balance for day-to-day transactions and, if he can spare some of it, it will not be much and he will sacrifice his liquidity only in consideration of a large and immediate gain — say, if he expects that the price of gold will be raised over the week-end. A decision to exchange dollars into other currencies is much more likely, because the cost of in-and-out trading is much smaller and the liquidity of other currencies not much lower even if only dollars were usable for the regular foreign transactions of the particular firm or bank.

Yet, under the arrangements in effect until March 17, 1968, both kinds of switch affected the gold stocks of the United States in a rather similar way. This resulted from a combination of two practices: (1) the arrangements of the Gold Pool provided for sales of monetary gold to private buyers whenever the demand in the London gold market was not fully met by supplies from private stocks and new production; 59 per cent of the wanted gold was supplied by the United States, the other 41 per cent by Germany, Italy, Belgium, Netherland, United Kingdom, and Switzerland. (2) Several of these countries had set upper limits to their holdings of dollars; as the proceeds of their sales of gold increased their dollar holdings, the collected dollars would sooner or later be presented to the authorities of the United States for conversion into gold.

Now, what effects can be expected if private dollar holders switch from dollars into francs, DM, lïre, or other strong currencies? The central banks issuing these currencies and acquiring the dollars may again find their dollar holdings increased beyond the limit and may seek their conversion into gold. Thus it seems that in both cases of private foreigners reducing their dollar balances, whether they want to replace them with another currency or with gold, the end-effect would be a loss of gold by the United States.

In March 1968, the seven countries of the Gold Pool agreed on a new policy. They will no longer supply gold to the London market, even if the market price of gold should rise as a result. Moreover, the six countries may allow their dollar holdings to increase; that is, they will not present surplus dollars for prompt conversion into gold. There is probably no commitment to this effect and certainly there is nothing that would commit other countries to refrain from asking the United States to surrender gold for dollars. A brief review of the past behavior of foreign monetary authorities regarding their holdings of gold and foreign exchange may be helpful in an appraisal of official attitudes.

Taking all noncommunist countries together, their official holdings of dollars increased steadily until the end of 1965, when they reached a peak of $15.9 billion. The decline that followed was quite modest: to $14.4 billion in September 1967. Focusing, however, on the industrial countries of Europe, we notice that they began earlier to reduce the foreign-exchange portion of their monetary reserves: at the end of 1964 they held $9.2 billion, a year later only $7.5 billion. In the same year they increased their gold holdings from $16.9 billion to $18.9 billion. France and Germany were leading in this switch of their monetary reserves. Germany had started a year ahead of all others, reducing her foreign-exchange holdings from $3.3 billion at the end of 1963 to $2.7 billion in 1964 and to $1.7 billion in March 1965, while increasing gold stocks from $3.8 billion to $4.4 billion in the same period. France reduced her foreign-exchange reserves from $1.4 billion at the end of 1964 to $0.8 billion in 1965 and $0.5 billion in 1966, building up her gold holdings from $3.7 billion at the end of 1964 to $4.7 billion a year later and $5.2 billion at the end of 1966. All these switches cut into the gold reserves of the United States, reducing them from $15.5 billion at the end of 1964 to $14.1 billion in 1965 and to $13.2 billion in 1966.

The reductions in dollar holdings by monetary authorities were halted when the situation became critical. Several countries, indeed, agreed to reverse the direction of change in the composition of their reserves. Leading among those that have increased their holdings of dollars are Germany and Italy. But this does not mean that the official holders of dollars have forever foresworn conversions into gold. One may assume that the authorities in practically all countries wish to avoid a crisis, the outcome of which cannot be predicted but is apt to be deleterious to most. Yet, if in some countries, in a moment of stress, the men in charge of international monetary affairs were to lose their heads, and a threat of a stampede for gold seemed imminent, official demands for conversions could become large enough for the United States to realize that the sale of gold cannot be continued.

In any case the double threat of the "dollar overhang" accumulated over many years and of the current "dollar overflow" from continuing payments deficits of the United States makes it difficult to be sanguine about the ability of this country to satisfy all potential official requests for gold.

The Gold Rush

Having talked about the dangers of gold hoarding by nervous dollar holders, I must now proceed to discuss private gold purchases by holders of other currencies.

Purchases of gold in the London market are paid in dollars. If those for whose accounts the gold is bought have no dollar balances, they first have to acquire dollars with whatever currencies they may have been holding — pounds, Swiss francs, rupees, kyats, bahts, wons, kips, piastres, or any other.[6] The results of an increased private demand for gold will differ according to whether it is met out of new production of gold; or is met out of monetary reserves under the arrangements of the Gold Pool (rescinded in March 1968); or results in a higher gold price in the free market.

Assume that the final buyers are Thais, paying in bahts, and that the sellers are South Africans, who want their proceeds in rands, to pay for the production cost of gold. There will therefore be a supply of bahts in search of dollars, a payment of dollars for gold, and a supply of dollars in search of rands. If both the baht and the rand are pegged in terms of dollars and, hence, the authorities of Thailand and South Africa intervene in the foreign-exchange markets, the dollar holdings of Bangkok will decrease and those of Johannesburg increase. If the adjustment process works, the balances of goods and services of the two countries will eventually adjust and show larger exports from Thailand and larger imports (matching the exports of commercial gold) into South Africa. The dollar, having served in the process as transactions currency, will not be affected either way.

Let us now see what happens if the new demand for gold cannot be met out of new production but, under gold-pool arrangements designed to stabilize the gold price in the free market, is met out of official reserves sold by monetary authorities. Assume that the final buyers are Indians, paying in rupees, and the sellers are the monetary authorities participating in the Gold Pool. I shall not go into the delicate question whether the Reserve Bank of India will furnish dollars to the rupee owners (whose demand for foreign exchange may come in a disguise that appears quite legitimate) or in what other ways dollars become available to them. The relevant part of the process is the loss of monetary gold. Under the old arrangements, the seven countries joined in the Gold Pool had shared the loss. The European central banks in this case would not necessarily have acquired additional dollars in exchange for their gold, since the private demand for dollar balances had not declined:

---

[6]The last five are the currencies of Burma, Thailand, Korea, Laos, and Vietnam.

it was the demand for rupee holdings that declined. If the Indian authorities stayed out of the picture, the rupees may have been offered at a price attractive enough for some people to buy them with dollars or other currencies, either to make purchases in India or even to hold the rupees temporarily for speculative reasons. The central banks supplying the gold might find their note circulation or demand deposits reduced or their dollar holdings increased. And eventually they would return such dollars to New York for gold. Thus, at least in part, the Indians' gold hoarding would have encroached on American gold stocks.

If enough statistical information were at hand, we could establish to what extent major scrambles for gold were associated with reductions in private foreign holdings of dollars. It would be important to know whether the tidal wave of private gold purchases in December 1967, which took $900 million from the American gold stocks within four weeks, left private foreign dollar holdings more or less unchanged or reduced by a similar amount. There had been earlier gold rushes, besides the gradual increases in private hoards. Thus, in 1960 additions to private gold stocks jumped by $311 million, or 68 per cent of the 1959 purchases, and in 1965, by $449 million, or 67 per cent of the 1964 purchases.[7] But we do not know whether private dollar holdings in those years reflected any "movements out of dollars."

One conclusion of these reflections is that, under the old gold-pool arrangements, private gold purchases could encroach upon the gold reserves of the United States even if the purchases were made by foreigners not holding dollars but using their own currencies to pay for the gold. Regardless of whether the gold rushes between December 1967 and March 1968 were associated with reductions in the demand for dollar balances or were financed with other currencies, the depletion of American gold holdings was too rapid for the authorities to stand by inactively. More than $2.4 billion worth

---

[7] These large jumps clearly refute the hypothesis, advanced by official and unofficial experts, that the increase in private purchases of gold is a nonspeculative, "structural" development. Nothing but speculation can explain the sudden leaps in 1960, 1965, and 1967.

of gold was lost within the three months, reducing the stocks to $10.5 billion. The decision by the members of the Gold Pool, on March 17, 1968, to halt sales to private parties and no longer to intervene in the London gold market was a sensible reaction. But what will now be the effects of private excess demand for gold?

Assume that speculators want to acquire more gold than is available from new production after the requirements of industrial and artistic users and traditional hoarders are satisfied. Without any sales out of monetary stocks, the sole source of supply for bullish speculators is gold relinquished by less bullish speculators. That is to say, the eager buyers will bid up the market price to a point at which less eager holders are willing to part with enough of their gold to meet the demand. Although dollars are used in the transactions, the position of the dollar in the exchange markets will not be affected if neither buyers nor sellers of the gold reduce or increase their dollar balances in the end. If the buyers have, at the outset, had currencies other than dollars, and had to buy dollars in order to buy gold, whereas the sellers, at the increased price of gold, hold on to the dollar proceeds, the dollar will be strengthened in the process and some central banks may have to sell dollars against their own currencies. Conversely, if the buyers have held dollars whereas the sellers want to hold their proceeds in other currencies, the dollar will be weakened and some central banks may have to acquire dollars under our system of fixed exchange rates.

It would be difficult to predict which of these three possibilities is the most likely to materialize — were it not for the continuing supply of additional dollars originating from the payments deficit of the United States. With this continuing deficit, one may expect that dollars, both from the current overflow and from the amassed overhang, will land in the hands of foreign monetary authorities and, through conversion, contribute to the further erosion of the gold position of the United States.

Cheap Advice

If the predicament is due chiefly to the deficits in the balance of payments and to a lack of confidence in the United States dollar, it requires no great wisdom to conclude that all will be well if balance and confidence are restored. The cheapest advice is to say that restoring balance will restore confidence and that therefore no more is needed than to remove the continuous overspending, overlending, and overinvesting by the United States.

External balance does not guarantee confidence in the sense of maintenance of a given volume of foreign dollar holdings. The foreign demand for dollar balances depends chiefly on the volume of dollar transactions for which working balances are needed. Any measures or policies that reduce the volume of foreign trade and payments may well reduce the foreign demand for private dollar holdings, and thus lead to further conversions and to American gold losses, even if the payments deficit (on liquidity basis) is reduced or removed. Moreover, "overspending, overlending, and overinvesting" are relative magnitudes, and absolute reductions in foreign spending, lending, and investing need not reduce, and may even increase, the relative oversize of the particular items in the balance of payments.

What can really be done to achieve a cure of the chronic imbalance of payments and to safeguard against crises of confidence?

Restoring Balance: Direct Controls

There are several ways of dealing with a deficit in the balance of payments: to finance it, suppress it through restrictions, try to remove it through real or financial correctives, or restore balance through real adjustment.

After 18 years of financing the deficit, the time has come to end it. Picking some conspicious deficit items in the balance of payments, the United States has decided to "take action" against these items, partly by means of direct controls and prohibitions. The government hopes the country will save at least $1 billion by a "mandatory program" to restrain direct investment abroad and to bring home larger portions of foreign earnings from past investments; another $500 million by a "tightened program" to restrain foreign lending by banks and other financial institutions; another $500 million by reducing "nonessential travel outside the Western

Hemisphere"; and again another $500 million by reducing the foreign-exchange cost of keeping troops in Europe.

Even if the new program succeeded in improving the balance of payments by $2.5 billion, it would still not *restore balance*. It would only *suppress imbalance,* and probably only temporarily. When the controls and restrictions are lifted, the deficit is apt to reappear in its full size. At best the reduction of the cost of keeping troops in Europe may turn out to be a continuing saving — either by bringing some of the troops home or by receiving compensatory payments from the NATO allies. All the other items, however, have to be regarded as regular flows, determined by underlying conditions such as levels of incomes and prices and rates of profit and capital formation. Such flows can be restricted or suppressed for a time but, if the underlying conditions are not altered, they will resume at the same or even increased strength as soon as the restrictions and prohibitions are taken off.

That the suppression of a deficit by use of police power does not restore "equilibrium" but merely conceals the symptoms of "disequilibrium," is relatively easy to grasp (though many manage to forget it). It is less easy to understand that the suppression of deficit items in amounts equal to the present deficit may yet fail to remove the deficit. The naive observer of the statistic of international transactions is inclined to assume that each reduction of a deficit item will be fully reflected in a reduction of the "over-all deficit." It takes hard intellectual work to comprehend the interdependence between the various items, to see, for example, why a reduction in the expenditures of American tourists abroad or a reduction in American direct investment abroad will to some extent result in increased imports and reduced exports of goods and services. These "feedbacks" may be large or small, but will rarely be zero. They can be zero only if the reduction in the flow of funds does not affect the use of funds either in the domestic or in the foreign market. Assume that an American, A, is prevented from lending his money to a foreigner, F; only if A then decides to sit on his money and not to spend, lend, or invest any part of it, and if F manages to disburse abroad exactly the same amount of money that he could have disbursed thanks to the receipt of A's funds, only then will imports and exports be unaffected by the financial corrective. In all probability, A will use some of his funds at home and F will have less to spend abroad, and the United States will have larger imports and smaller exports as a result.[8]

Restoring Balance: Partial Devaluation

Besides direct controls, various measures have been introduced to alter the ratios between selected domestic and foreign values. These measures are designed, by changing the basis of economic calculation, to divert purchases from foreign to domestic markets. They can most conveniently be regarded as disguised, partial devaluations of the dollar.

First, the dollar used for military expenditures abroad was devalued when the officials in charge were instructed to "buy American" whenever the cost was not more than 50 per cent above the cost in foreign currency calculated at the official exchange rate. Next came the concealed devaluation of the dollar used by recipients of foreign aid; they were forced to buy in the United States, even if they could have bought elsewhere at lower prices. As a result of the tied purchases the worth of the aid-dollar was reduced by about 25 per cent. The third partial devaluation was that of the dollar used for purchases of foreign securities: the so-called interest-equalization tax was equivalent to an increase in the price of foreign currencies by 15 per cent. The proposals made early in 1968 include a devaluation of the tourist's dollar by means of special taxes on travel expenditures outside the Western Hemisphere.

All such selective correctives through partial devaluation are inequitable, discriminatory, and inefficient, although they are superior to direct controls in that they work by means of price incentives and disincentives and leave the market essentially free.

---

[8] Feedbacks and other offsetting repercussions will also prevent the end of the war in Vietnam from ending the deficit in foreign payments. Military spending abroad may be replaced by foreign aid — as has been promised — or exports from the United States will decline. Military spending at home may be replaced by other domestic expenditures — many outlays in the war against poverty having been postponed — and if so imports will fail to decline.

They all invite substitution, evasion, and circumvention; they discriminate against some sectors and in favor of others, distort the structure of prices, and induce misallocation of productive resources. Usually, they are also incapable of effecting their purpose. For, while they improve particular items in the balance of payments, they worsen others, partly because of the substitution of purchases for which the dollar is not devalued, partly because of foreign and domestic repercussions from the reduction of purchases for which the value of the dollar is reduced.

If the disguised devaluations of the dollar were uniform — for example, by means of proportional taxes on all imports and subsidies on all exports of goods, services, and securities — they might work indiscriminately; but the administrative difficulties would be serious. While theoretically taxes and subsidies could be used in lieu of a uniform alteration of exchange rates, in practice they would amount to a system of multiple exchange rates with plenty of bureaucratic bungling and high rewards for cheating and bribing.

I conclude that selective measures to remove the deficit, whether they are real correctives (designed to affect the flow of goods and services) or financial correctives (operating on the flow of capital funds) are not likely to achieve sustainable balance. Only real adjustment is likely to accomplish that.

Restoring Balance: Real Adjustment

In the process of real adjustment relative prices and incomes are changed in such a way that the allocation of real resources and the international flows of goods and services are altered sufficiently to improve the current account so as to make it match the balance on capital account and unilateral payments. I distinguish three approaches: aggregate-demand adjustment, cost-and-price adjustment, and exchange-rate adjustment. The first two are practically inseparable, because demand adjustment works largely through changes in costs and prices, and cost-and-price adjustments cannot, as a rule, be achieved without demand adjustment.

Aggregate-demand adjustment implies income deflation and

less employment in the deficit country and/or income-and-price inflation in the surplus country. Since excessive expansion of demand in the deficit country has often contributed to the emergence or persistence of the payments deficit, stopping the inflation is, in such instances, the first and most urgent recommendation. But merely disinflationary policies cannot accomplish full adjustment when the surplus countries likewise desist from inflating aggregate demand. Only if these countries allowed their income and price levels to rise would the prevention of income-and-price inflation in the deficit country initiate a process of real adjustment, leading gradually to restoration of external balance as the "demand pull" in foreign countries washed their surpluses away.

While halting or containing the inflation in the deficit country is not yet a sufficient condition for real adjustment, it is a necessary condition for preventing the deficit from getting bigger. Thus, fiscal and monetary restraint — higher taxes, reduced expenditures, tighter credit — are imperative, simply to keep the imbalance of payments from getting worse. Yet, to prescribe the same orthodox medicine in doses large enough to induce full adjustment would mean to expose the country to great risks. Stopping an inflation is one thing; forcing a deflation is another. In the absence of inflation abroad, real adjustment of the existing imbalance would require net deflation in the deficit country, at a probably exorbitant social and economic cost, which no government is willing to impose on the country.

The third approach to real adjustment — exchange-rate adjustment — is also resisted by governments. The United States regards it as practically impossible, partly because of some past promises and commitments, partly because of the role of its currency in international affairs. The trading partners of the United States regard this kind of adjustment as undesirable, and perhaps intolerable, chiefly because it would weaken the competitive position of their industries. Exchange-rate adjustment may, nevertheless, prove to be the only practicable way out. However, it can become practicable only by courses of action not yet sufficiently examined. Some of them will be considered here, but only after an analysis of the problem of confidence.

Restoring Confidence: Five Approaches

Confidence in a currency, or any liquid asset, is always relative, namely, compared with some alternative asset; the problem is the likelihood of massive switches between alternative assets held. Economists have long known that a currency system with two moneys, such as gold and silver coins, with fixed rates of conversion is very unstable and should not be tolerated (Gresham's law).

The problem of increased or reduced confidence in the dollar lies in its convertibility into gold. Changes in expectations regarding the relative scarcity of the two assets lead to massive switches, which in turn may result in major disturbances of world monetary affairs. Switches from dollars to gold may, if convertibility is maintained, destroy large amounts of monetary reserves and induce deflation and unemployment in several countries. Switches from gold into dollars would increase monetary reserves, as the disgorging of private gold hoards creates additional reserves of commercial banks as well as additional cash balances of individuals and firms, which induces inflation of prices and incomes everywhere.

Traditionalists are fond of repeating that confidence is lost only when governments have misbehaved, and that convertibility into gold enforces discipline. Both statements are, to put it mildly, exaggerated. Expectations of lower production and rising industrial use of gold may lead to a large speculative demand for gold even if the creation of dollars has not been excessive by any traditional standards. And the fear of losing reserves of gold has rarely in modern times kept monetary authorities from engaging in monetary expansion when they wanted to promote employment and growth. The allegiance to gold exerts no discipline, it merely creates guilt feelings.

The traditional advice to the monetary authorities anxious to restore confidence in the dollar is that they make the dollar scarce. However, when popular belief in a future scarcity of gold is widespread, it would take severe deflationary measures by the United States to achieve a matching scarcity of the dollar. It would be downright madness to accept the prescription of a stiff dose of deflation.

The most strongly advocated recommendation is to increase the official price of gold to take account of the expected relative scarcities.[9] A sharp increase in the official dollar price of gold could restore confidence in the devalued dollar for a few years, but only at a very high cost. One of the noneconomic cost factors would be the humiliation of the nation which, breaching the solemn promises of its three last presidents — Eisenhower, Kennedy, and Johnson — would "cheat" its best friends (who have believed the assurances and continued to hold dollars) and reward those who have been least friendly. The economic cost would mainly come from the world inflation induced by the monetization of gold profits. For even if the official profits from a revaluation of gold were to be safely sterilized, the profits of private hoarders and speculators would be monetized, their sales creating new bank reserves and new cash — perhaps to the tune of some twenty billion dollars — with no chance for any monetary policies that could offset this outpouring of new money. The point is that speculators in the last eight or ten years have purchased between $10 billion and $15 billion worth of gold at $35 an ounce and are waiting for the price to be increased. If the price were doubled, their treasure would be worth at least $20 billion (to use the lower estimate) and this would be the amount of national currencies which central banks would have to create in payment for the dishoarded gold. The reserves of commercial banks would rise

---

[9] The expectations of speculators are based on the assumption that the monetary gold stocks will never be released. If speculators realized that these reserves could eventually be employed as a "buffer stock" to fill gaps between production and private demand, they would sell gold, rather than buy. A sober estimate looks like this: industrial and artistic uses of gold absorbed about $500 million worth in 1967, and purchases by traditional hoarders about the same amount. Production (not counting the output in communist countries) was roughly $1,500 million, the surplus of $500 million being bought by speculators. If this surplus were purchased neither by speculators nor by monetary authorities, the resulting glut would depress the market price far below the present level. One may reckon, however, that purchases by industrial and artistic users and by traditional hoarders will increase from year to year, and production will fall, so that the excess supply may vanish and eventually give way to an excess demand. Still, since the present stocks held by speculators plus the buffer stocks of the authorities are at least $55 billion, they could cover 55 years of the present private use, even if production fell to zero!

by the same amount and would create additional lending power of some $100 billion, a truly frightening inflationary potential. The inconsistency of the gold-price boosters is amazing: they praise the gold standard for its alleged disciplinary anti-inflationary effects, but are willing to subject the world to a huge inflation in the process of restoring gold to its long-lost importance in the monetary system.

Besides these two recipes — one to make the dollar scarcer by deflationary policies, the other to make gold more abundant by doubling its price — several other proposals have been made, mainly for schemes to prevent official switching from dollars to gold. Three approaches can be distinguished: (1) "locking in" the dollars in the official reserves of the nations under so-called harmonization agreements, (2) taking out the dollars from official reserves by having them turned in to an international conversion account in exchange for deposits that are generally recognized as reserves, and (3) terminating both the convertibility of official dollar holdings into gold and the convertibility of gold into dollars. All these approaches would face strong political resistance, but this is true for every measure that might do the job.

Restoring Confidence: Locking-In and Pooling Agreements

Harmonization agreements would bind countries to hold a minimum ratio of their total reserves in the form of dollar assets. Alternatively, since a fixed ratio would imply annual increases in official dollar holdings (which may be unacceptable to some countries), the minimum holdings could be stipulated in absolute amounts. As a consideration for the promise to hold the balances, an exchange-value or gold-value guarantee may have to be given for official holdings. Such an agreement, unless it included additional provisions, would fail to guard against massive sales of dollars to central banks in the case of private asset switching (dollars into gold or into other currencies) and in the case of continuing deficits in the payments balance of the United States. Moreover, the scheme fails to provide for the possibility of a continuing excess demand for gold by processors, hoarders, and speculators. One way of dealing with this problem is the separation of official transactions at an official price from private transactions at a free-market price — the system introduced in March 1968. Another way would be to maintain a uniform price of gold, which would require a combination of a gold-selling agreement with a dollar-holding agreement among monetary authorities.

To remove reserve currencies from national monetary reserves by having them deposited with an international reserve pool has been part of several proposals, including the Keynes Plan of 1943 and the various plans by Triffin, Bernstein, and Maudling. These plans have differed in their generality, for example, on whether all of the existing overhang of dollars and pounds should be turned in or only amounts that the holders consider excessive, and whether the national authorities, having gotten rid of their existing holdings or excess holdings, should be allowed to acquire new dollars or pounds. To deal with the existing overhang but allow new accumulations of reserve currencies would seem inconsistent. A "final solution" of the problem of confidence would have to exclude future accumulations of reserve currencies after funding the accumulations of the past.

The removal of reserve currencies from national reserves to an international agency would leave the gold problem unsettled. To have a two-ring circus with private gold acrobatics in one ring and official gold clownery in the other, with the official gold dispersed among a hundred reserve-holding countries, all of whom would also hold presumably gold-value-guaranteed deposits in the international agency — this would hardly be a definitive solution of international monetary affairs. If the private price of gold differed substantially from the official price, leaks would be likely to develop from one circulation to the other. The ratio between exchange-pool deposits and gold in the monetary reserves would differ from country to country and problems of differential confidence in these two reserve assets might arise. Nothing, therefore, would be more sensible than to call for a central gold pool; but rather than setting up a separate gold pool, it would seem much more logical to have the same international agency corral all the monetary gold as well as all the existing reserve-currency holdings.

Since one of the predicaments in the present situation is the danger that dollars are converted into gold and thereby disappear as monetary reserves, this solution — that both the dollars and the gold are deposited in the same pool and that the deposit liabilities (or certificates) of the pool become the major reserve asset of the national authorities — is so rational, so cogent, that to me it seems compelling. The two problems — of safeguarding against official switches between dollars and gold and of providing for future developments in the supply and demand for gold — could hardly be solved in a neater way than by pooling all, or almost all, official holdings of both types of reserve assets. Gold and national reserve currencies would simultaneously disappear from the reserves of national monetary authorities, replaced by deposits with a conversion account (reserve-settlement account) of the International Monetary Fund.

One may wonder whether countries could be persuaded to accept such a comprehensive solution. The United States could free itself of persistent conversion headaches by transferring its entire gold stock (about $10.5 billion in March 1968) to the IMF and then using the resulting deposits as its major reserve. Germany, Italy, and other countries holding both dollars and gold could avoid awkward external and internal political pressures regarding the most appropriate division of their reserves between non-interest-earning gold and non-value-guaranteed dollars by exchanging both for interest-bearing and exchange-value-guaranteed deposit claims against the Fund. France, now holding chiefly gold, might find the solution acceptable if the Fund agreed to keep some of its gold in vaults on French soil, if no credits, investments, loans, or overdrafts were to be extended in connection with the scheme — the SDR-facility alone taking care of the provision of additional reserves — and if all participants agreed not to acquire any national currencies as part of their official reserves beyond working balances of strictly limited size.[10]

---

[10]To make it quite clear: only those dollars and pounds that are held in national monetary reserves when the conversion account is established are eligible for exchange into the new reserve asset. There can be no later additions, either from present private holdings or from later payments deficits of the United States or United Kingdom.

The new conversion account (or reserve-settlement account) of the Fund could also assume the function of dealing with the problem of nonmonetary gold. In principle it would be possible to leave the gold market completely free, the Fund neither selling nor buying, no matter what price gold would fetch in the free market. In this case one might expect the price of gold, perhaps after a few months with higher quotations, to fall considerably below the present price of $35 an ounce. For there would probably be substantial dishoarding of gold by disappointed speculators, and industrial demand would still be far below the volume of new gold production. After a few years industrial uses of gold would increase enough to exceed the private supply, and then the price could go above $35. By that time even the most conservative central bankers and financial authorities would have learned that the large monetary gold stock kept buried by the international agency was serving absolutely no purpose. The question would then be asked why one should allow gold permanently to be withheld from productive uses and whether it was not more intelligent to release it from the monetary concentration camp.

Instead of letting the price of gold in the free market first fall far below and later rise far above the present official price, the Fund could operate a buffer stock, taking over the task which national monetary authorities have carried out for so long. (This collective buffer stock accumulated gold for hundreds of years and began selling only in 1965.) If the Fund is to buy and sell gold, it should perhaps maintain a pair of prices — buying, say, at $34 or below and selling at $36 or above — so that it would have a source of income besides the interest earned on the dollar and sterling assets taken over from national monetary authorities. Gold-mining interests would surely plead for higher prices or for postponement of any sales from the pooled reserves. The decision would not be of great consequence once it is settled that there can be no purchases for monetary reserves at any increased price.

Still another function could be assigned to the conversion account (reserve-settlement account) of the Fund: to devise a quasi-automatic adjustment of the exchange rates for the currencies of the participating countries. The parities of all currencies might be stated in terms of Fund Units. Any country losing reserves at a fast rate over an extended period might have the exchange value of its currency lowered in small steps, and any country gaining reserves at a fast rate over an extended period might have the exchange value of its currency raised in small steps, not exceeding 3 per cent per year. Alternatively, the Fund might adopt the device of "band flexibility" of exchange rates, that is, a widening of the permissible margin of rate fluctuations from the present 1 per cent to 3 or 4 per cent above and below par. The best solution, however, would combine the "crawling peg" with the "wider band" and allow the use of a "movable band" of exchange rates. It need not apply to all currencies, but only to those of countries or blocs of countries that do not choose to coordinate their fiscal and monetary policies with those of other countries (or blocs) and thus to subordinate their domestic objectives to that of maintaining external balance. The technique of the movable band could furnish the international monetary system with the only reliable and economical adjustment mechanism for countries in which adjustments of incomes and prices are not tolerated.

However, it would not be necessary to burden international negotiations at this time with such controversial questions: the men in the seats of power at present seem unwilling to consider proposals of this sort. Their successors in a few years may be more open-minded. It may be wiser, therefore, to confine the agenda for immediate negotiations to the most urgent points. The most urgent is to avert the danger of having several billion dollars of existing monetary reserves destroyed through the exchange of official dollar holdings for official gold holdings.

Restoring Confidence: Cutting the Link

Some of the experts in international monetary affairs tell us that nothing is negotiable at the moment. The governments, so we are told, will not, after the years of negotiating the SDR facility, sit down again to negotiate additional reforms, least of all, reforms as radical as the removal of gold and reserve currencies from national reserves. If this warning is correct, the next alternative may have to be considered, though it is a less desirable one, because, as a unilateral action, it offends the spirit of international cooperation.

The conversion of official dollar holdings into gold leaves the reserves of the switchers unchanged — they will have gold in place of the dollars — but reduces the gross reserves of the United States — the loss of gold being compensated merely by a reduction of dollar liabilities. This destruction of gross reserves is harmful if it induces deflation and/or restrictions on the flow of goods and capital; it would not be so harmful if the losers of gold — the United States — did not take restrictive measures.

Equanimity or indifference vis-à-vis the loss of gold can be created if gold reserves are no longer needed for anything — neither to meet internal legal requirements or external moral obligations nor to safeguard the maintenance of fixed exchange rates. These changes in the role of gold in the United States can be produced by cutting the link between the dollar and gold, that is, by terminating the rule that the United States will purchase gold whenever offered and will sell gold to monetary authorities that hold dollars.

In view of promises made and expectations fostered by frequent declarations of the United States government, it would be decent if the United States offered to give up all its gold to monetary authorities that wanted to reduce their holdings of dollars. In order to assure a fair distribution, it could first invite each of them to state the amount of dollars for which they wanted gold. Would the gold stock of the United States — of less than $11 billion — be large enough to meet the official demand? The foreign monetary authorities hold almost $16 billion, but surely they would not want to invest all their dollars in gold. All of them need dollars as working balances and as intervention balances; many of them are anxious to have interest-earning assets in their monetary reserves; and several of them need dollars as compensating balances against American bank loans. The desire to keep dollars would be increased if it were understood that the United States would in the future not purchase any new gold and not repurchase any of the gold now sold. The point of these considerations is not that we should care how much gold the United States would retain, but rather whether the present stock would suffice to meet the demands.

After the United States made the great decision to terminate convertibility between dollar and gold, all further decisions about the relations among currencies would be left to other countries. It would be for them, and not for the United States, to decide the value of the dollar in their foreign exchange markets. One can imagine four types of decisions.

1. Some countries may decide to keep the present exchange rates between their currencies and the dollar unchanged; in this case, they would have to purchase all dollars offered in the market and to increase their dollar holdings if the dollar should continue to be in excess supply.

2. Some countries may decide not to increase their holdings of dollars and, instead, to reduce the price they pay for dollars offered to them; in other words, they may decide to raise the dollar value of their own currencies.

3. Some countries, unwilling to increase their dollar holdings and uncertain about the right price to pay for the dollar, may decide to let their exchange rate float, against the dollar and other currencies that remain linked with the dollar; in other words, they may let exchange rates be determined by supply and demand in a free market.

4. Some countries may be anxious not to allow the dollar to be devalued or depreciated, because this could hurt some of their industries; they might therefore continue to purchase dollars at the present exchange rate whenever an excess supply arises from transactions in goods and services, but they might refuse dollars that originate from imports of capital. This would amount to multiple exchange rates, a system workable only in connection with foreign-exchange controls.

The United States should gladly accept any of the first three possibilities. The first one would amount to the willingness of other countries to help finance its payments deficit. The second and third would greatly aid in the process of adjustment; indeed, it might be the only practicable approach to adjustment. Only the fourth possibility would be deplorable, but not more so than the restrictions which the United States itself has been imposing. If there are to be restrictions on the movement of capital, they had better be imposed by the countries unwilling to receive capital than by the country able to supply it.

The termination of gold convertibility would not change the role of the dollar as international transactions currency. The dollar may even continue as reserve currency for, while some monetary authorities may decide to sell their dollars, others may prefer to increase their dollar holdings. The present threat to stability, the possibility of massive switches at a fixed conversion rate, would no longer exist. The use of the dollar as international trade currency would not be affected at all. The dollar remains the most stable of all currencies and the most useful of all currencies (in the sense that it can draw on the largest reservoir of goods). As long as its purchasing power over goods and services is secure, the dollar will serve international trade and finance; its convertibility in gold is immaterial for this function.

One may ask what advantage this drastic action at this time may have over a policy of temporizing. The chief difference, from a realistic point of view, is between taking the step now or two or three years from now. To defer it, is to live under restrictions and under the constant threat of crises of confidence, each crisis bringing new and more stringent restrictions.

The Relation to the SDR Scheme

The most disconcerting thought is that unilateral action by the United States may so seriously offend the spirit of international cooperation that the pretty solution that was found for the liquidity problem might be ruined, or at least tabled for an indefinite period. If this were to happen, it would clearly show the mistake we have made in giving priority to the problem of liquidity and disregarding the problems of confidence and adjustment. It would be most unfortunate to have the hard work of several years come to nought.

Such a course of events is by no means inevitable. Responsible governments may reflect on the possible developments and realize that a failure to negotiate collective actions solving the problems of confidence and adjustment might jeopardize the successful solution of the liquidity problem. With this prospect in mind, they may overcome their disinclination to resume their efforts toward a cooperative completion of the entire agenda.

Now that the United States has imposed mandatory restrictions on capital movements and proposes to impose restriction on purchases of foreign services, the blessings of a scheme to create liquidity seem less promising. The main justification — perhaps the only one that really counts — of the creation of international reserves is the avoidance of restrictions. If it takes restrictions to activate a plan for the creation of reserves, the whole idea is defiled.

How sad that intelligent people work hard to find suitable means for achieving desirable ends, then promote the means as if they were ends in themselves, and begin pursuing them with instruments that negate the original ends.

Appendix A

Outline of a Facility
Based on Special Drawing Rights
in the International Monetary Fund

Introduction

The facility described in this Outline is intended to meet the need, as and when it arises, for a supplement to existing reserve assets. It is to be established within the framework of the Fund and, therefore, by an Amendment of the Fund's Articles. Provisions relating to some of the topics in this Outline could be included in By-laws adopted by the Board of Governors or Rules and Regulations adopted by the Executive Directors rather than in the Amendment.

I. Establishment of a Special Drawing Account in the Fund

(a) An Amendment to the Articles will establish a Special Drawing Account through which all the operations relating to special drawing rights will be carried out. The purposes of the facility will be set forth in the introductory section of the Amendment.

(b) The operations of and resources available under the Special Drawing Account will be separate from the operations of the present Fund which will be referred to as the General Account.

(c) Separate provisions will be included in the Amendment for withdrawal from or liquidation of the Special Drawing Account; Article XVI, Section 2, and Schedules D and E on withdrawal and liquidation will continue to apply as they do at present to the General Account of the Fund.

II. Participants and Other Holders

1. *Participants.* Participation in the Special Drawing Account will be open to any member of the Fund that undertakes the obligations of the Amendment. A member's quota in the Fund will be the same for the purposes of both the General and the Special Drawing Accounts of the Fund.

2. *Holding by General Account.* The General Account will be authorized to hold and use special drawing rights.

III. Allocation of Special Drawing Rights

1. *Principles for decisions.* The Special Drawing Account will allocate special drawing rights in accordance with the provisions of the Amendment. Special considerations applicable to the first decision to allocate special drawing rights, as well as the principles on which all decisions to allocate special drawing rights will be based, will be included in the introductory section of the Amendment and, to the extent necessary, in a Report explaining the Amendment.

2. *Basic period and rate of allocation.* The following provisions will apply to any decision to allocate special drawing rights:

(i) The decision will prescribe a basic period during which special drawing rights will be allocated at specified intervals. The period will normally be five years in length, but the Fund may decide that any basic period will be of different duration. The first basic period will begin on the effective date of the first decision to allocate special drawing rights.

(ii) The decision will also prescribe the rate or rates at which special drawing rights will be allocated during the basic period. Rates will be expressed as a percentage, uniform for all participants, of quotas on the date specified in the decision.

3. *Procedure for decisions*

(a) Any decision on the basic period for, timing of, or rate of allocation of special drawing rights will be taken by the Board of Governors on the basis of a proposal by the Managing Director concurred in by the Executive Directors.

(b) Before formulating any proposal, the Managing Director after having satisfied himself that the considerations referred to in III.1 have been met, will conduct such consultations as will enable him to ascertain that there is broad support among participants for the allocation of special drawing rights at the proposed rate and for the proposed basic period.

(c) The Managing Director will make proposals with respect to the allocation of special drawing rights: (i) within sufficient time before the end of a basic period; (ii) in the circumstances of III.4; (iii) within six months after the Board of Governors or the Executive Directors request that he make a proposal. The Managing Director will make a proposal for the first basic period when he is of the opinion that there is broad support among the participants to start the allocation of special drawing rights.

(d) The Executive Directors will review both the operations of the Special Drawing Account and the adequacy of global reserves as part of their annual report to the Board of Governors.

4. *Change in rate of allocation or basic period.* If there are unexpected major developments which make it desirable to change the rate at which further special drawing rights are to be allocated for a basic period, (i) the rate may be increased or decreased, or (ii) the basic period may be terminated and a different rate of allocation adopted for a new basic period. Paragraph III.3 will apply to such changes.

5. *Voting majority*

(a) For decisions on the basic period for, timing of, amount and rate of allocation of special drawing rights, an 85 per cent majority of the voting power of participants shall be required.

(b) Notwithstanding (a) above, the decisions to decrease the rate of allocation of special drawing rights for the remainder of the basic period will be taken by a simple majority of the voting power of participants.

6. *Opting out*

The Amendment will include provisions that will prescribe to what extent a participant will be required initially to receive special drawing rights, but will stipulate that beyond any such amount a participant that does not vote in favor of a decision to allocate special drawing rights may elect not to receive them under that decision.

IV. Cancellation of Special Drawing Rights

The principles set forth in III relating to the procedure and voting for the allocation of special drawing rights will be applicable, with appropriate modifications, to the cancellation of such rights.

V. Use of Special Drawing Rights

1. *Right to use special drawing rights*

(a) A participant will be entitled, in accordance with the provisions of V, to use special drawing rights to acquire an equivalent amount of a currency convertible in fact. A participant which thus provides currency will receive an equivalent amount of special drawing rights.

(b) Within the framework of such rules and regulations as the Fund may adopt, a participant may obtain the currencies referred to in (a) either directly from another participant or through the Special Drawing Account.

(c) Except as indicated in V.3(c), a participant will be expected to use its special drawing rights only for balance of payments needs or in the light of developments in its total reserves and not for the sole purpose of changing the composition of its reserves.

(d) The use of special drawing rights will not be subject to prior challenge on the basis of this expectation, but the Fund may make representations to any participant which, in the Fund's judgment, has failed to observe the expectation, and may direct drawings to such participant to the extent of such failure.

2. *Provision of currency*

A participant's obligation to provide currency will not extend beyond a point at which its holdings of special drawing rights in excess of the net cumulative amount of such rights allocated to it are equal to twice that amount. However, a participant may provide currency, or agree with the Fund to provide currency, in excess of this limit.

3. *Selection of participants to be drawn upon*

The Fund's rules and instructions relating to the participants from which currencies should be acquired by users of special drawing rights will be based on the following main general principles, supplemented by such principles as the Fund may find desirable from time to time:

(a) Normally, currencies will be acquired from participants that have a sufficiently strong balance of payments and reserve position, but this will not preclude the possibility that currency will be acquired from participants with strong reserve positions even though they have moderate balance of payments deficits.

(b) The Fund's primary criterion will be to seek to approach over time equality, among the participants indicated from time to time by the criteria in (a) above, in the ratios of their holdings of special drawing rights, or such holdings in excess of net cumulative allocations thereof, to total reserves.

(c) In addition, the Fund will, in its rules and instructions, provide for such use of special drawing rights, either directly between participants or through the intermediary of the Special Drawing Account, as will promote voluntary reconstitution and reconstitution under V.4.

(d) Subject to the provisions of V.1(c), a participant may use its special drawing rights to purchase balances of its currency held by another participant, with the agreement of the latter.

4. *Reconstitution*

(a) Members that use their special drawing rights will incur an obligation to reconstitute their position in accordance with principles which will take account of the amount and the duration of the use. These principles will be laid down in rules and regulations of the Fund.

(b) The rules for reconstitution of drawings made during the first basic period will be based on the following principles:

(i) The average net use, taking into account both use below and holdings above its net cumulative allocation, made by a participant of its special drawing rights calculated on the basis of the preceding five years, shall not exceed 70 per cent of its average net cumulative allocation during this period. Reconstitution under this subparagraph (i) will be brought about through the mechanism of transfers, by the Fund directing drawings correspondingly.

(ii) Participants will pay due regard to the desirability of pursuing over time a balanced relationship between their holdings of special drawing rights and other reserves.

(c) Reconstitution rules will be reviewed before the end of the first and of each subsequent period and new rules will be adopted, if necessary. If new rules are not adopted for a basic period, the rules for the preceding period shall apply unless it is decided to abrogate reconstitution rules. The same majority as is required for decisions on the basic period, timing of, or rate of allocation of special drawing rights will be required for decisions to adopt, amend, or abrogate reconstitution rules. Any amendment in the rules will govern the reconstitution of drawings made after the effective date of the amendment, unless otherwise decided.

VI. Interest and Maintenance of Gold Value

(a) *Interest*. A moderate rate of interest will be paid in special drawing rights on holdings of special drawing rights. The cost of this interest will be assessed against all participants in proportion to net cumulative allocations of special drawing rights to them.

(b) *Maintenance of gold value.* The unit of value for expressing special drawing rights will be equal to 0.888671 gram of fine gold. The rights and obligations of participants and of the Special Drawing Account will be subject to an absolute maintenance of gold value or to provisions similar to Article IV, Section 8, of the Fund's Articles.

VII. Functions of Fund Organs and Voting

1. *Exercise of powers.* The decisions taken with respect to the Special Drawing Account, and the supervision of its operations, will be carried out by the Board of Governors, the Executive Directors, the Managing Director, and the staff of the Fund. Certain powers, and in particular those relating to the adoption of decisions concerning the allocation, cancellation, and certain aspects of the use of special drawing rights, will be reserved to the Board of Governors. All other powers, except those specifically granted to other organs, will be vested in the Board of Governors which will be able to delegate them to the Executive Directors.

2. *Voting.* Except as otherwise provided in the Amendment, all decisions pertaining to the Special Drawing Account will be taken by a majority of votes cast. The precise formula for the voting power of participants, which will include basic and weighted votes, and possibly the adjustment of voting power in relation to the use of special drawing rights, will be the subject of later consideration.

VIII. General Provisions

1. *Collaboration.* Participants will undertake to collaborate with the Fund in order to facilitate the proper functioning and effective use of special drawing rights within the international monetary system.

2. *Nonfulfillment of obligations*

(a) If the Fund finds that a participant has failed to fulfill its obligations to provide currency in accordance with the Amendment, the Fund may suspend the right of the participant to use its special drawing rights.

(b) If the Fund finds that a participant has failed to fulfill any other obligation under the Amendment, the Fund may suspend the participant's right to use any special drawing rights allocated to, or acquired by, it after the suspension.

(c) Suspension under (a) or (b) above will not affect a participant's obligation to provide currency in accordance with the Amendment.

(d) The Fund may at any time terminate a suspension under (a) or (b) above.

3. *Accounts.* All changes in holdings of special drawing rights will take effect when recorded in the accounts of the Special Drawing Account.

IX. Entry into Force

The Amendment would enter into force in accordance with the terms of Article XVII of the Fund's Articles.

Appendix B

The Articles of Agreement
of the International Monetary Fund
as adopted in 1944 and amended in 1968

The original Articles of Agreement adopted at Bretton Woods in 1944 consist of an Introductory Article, twenty Articles, numbered I to XX (most of them subdivided into several Sections), and five Schedules, lettered A to E.

The amendment proposed in 1968 modifies the Introductory Article, Articles I, III, IV, V, VI, XII, XVIII, and XIX, and Schedule B; inserts a new Section in Article V; changes the title of Article XX (from "Final Provisions" to "Inaugural Provisions"); and adds twelve new Articles, XXI to XXXII, and four new Schedules, F to I.

The major modifications of the original articles are described in Appendix C, and the full text of the new articles and schedules are reproduced in Appendix D. For purposes of easy reference the titles of all articles, sections, and schedules are enumerated here:

List of Articles and Sections

Introductory Article

   I. Purposes

  II. Membership
    1. Original members
    2. Other members

 III. Quotas and Subscriptions
    1. Quotas
    2. Adjustment of quotas
    3. Subscriptions: time, place and form of payment
    4. Payments when quotas are changed
    5. Substitution of securities for currency

 IV. Par Values of Currencies
    1. Expression of par values
    2. Gold purchases based on par values
    3. Foreign exchange dealings based on parity
    4. Obligations regarding exchange stability
    5. Changes in par values
    6. Effect of unauthorized changes
    7. Uniform changes in par values
    8. Maintenance of gold value of the Fund's assets
    9. Separate currencies within a member's territories

List of Schedules

Appendix C

Proposed Modifications of
Original Articles of Agreement

The resolution adopted by the Board of Governors at the Twenty-Second Annual Meeting at Rio de Janeiro in September 1967 proposed amendments of the Articles of Agreement, not only for the purpose of establishing the new facility on the basis of the Outline, but also to provide "improvements in the present rules and practices of the Fund based on developments in world economic conditions and the experience of the Fund since the adoption of the [original] Articles of Agreement."

The proposed modifications, according to a report by the Executive Directors, relate to

"certain quota increases and associated matters; uniform proportionate changes in par values and the maintenance of the gold value of the Fund's assets in the event that such changes in par values are made; the use of the Fund's resources in the gold tranche, including use for capital transfers; a limitation on the Fund's power to introduce new facilities in the General Account for the unconditional use of the Fund's resources; the rules on repurchase under Article V, Section 7; the payment of a remuneration to members whose currencies are held by the Fund in amounts less than 75 per cent of quota; the distribution of net income; and the interpretation of the Articles of Agreement. The modifications in Articles I, III, V, VI, XII, XVIII, and XIX, and in Schedule B, which are included in the Proposed Amendment, are intended to give effect to these changes."

Several of the modifications serve only to make new or stiffer requirements for qualified-majority voting. In some instances, instead of an 80 per cent majority, as required in the original articles, an 85 per cent majority is required by the amendment. This relates specifically to quota changes as a result of the "general review of quotas" which the Fund is to conduct "at intervals of not more than five years" (Article III, Section 2); and to decisions dealing with the payment of increases in quotas, particularly in situations in which a member may be permitted to pay less than 25 per cent of its additional subscription in gold, decisions previously made by the Executive Directors by a majority of votes cast (Article III, Section 4). In some matters, an 85 per cent majority will be needed where the original articles required only a simple majority and the approval by those members that have 10 per cent or more of the total of quotas. This change relates to a decision to make a uniform proportionate change in par values (Article IV, Section 7). The same 85 per cent majority will be needed for a decision to waive the maintenance of the gold value of the Fund's assets in the event of a uniform proportionate change in par value (Article IV, Section 8). On certain matters, decisions which under the original articles could be delegated to the Executive Directors, will now be reserved to the Board of Governors.

Several modifications are designed to adapt the original Articles to the establishment of the new SDR facility. For example, the Introductory Article, which has had only one sentence, will now have three paragraphs, referring chiefly to the division of Fund operations into those of the General Account and those of the Special Drawing Account. The establishment of the new facility is also reflected in certain changes in the access to the resources of the Fund (General Account). Thus, the Fund will no longer be able to grant *"de facto* automaticity"* to requests for purchases other than "gold tranche purchases" (Article V, Section 3). The provisions concerning "Repurchase by a member of its currency held by the Fund" will be changed in several respects, some of which reflect the future availability of SDR's (Article V, Section 7). A new provision is to give equal treatment to holders of positions in the General Account and in the Special Drawing Account. Since participants in the new scheme will receive interest on their excess holdings of SDR's, members are to receive a remuneration, normally one and one-half per cent per annum and payable in gold or in the member's own currency, for those parts of their normal currency subscriptions which the Fund has used in its operations. In the words proposed, the remuneration will be "on the amount by which seventy-five per cent of a member's quota exceeded the average of the Fund's holdings of the member's currency, provided that no account shall be taken of holdings in excess of seventy-five per cent of quota" (Article V, Section 9).

A number of modifications are designed to make present practices of the Fund, which have evolved over the years in sometimes extensive interpretation of the original articles, perfectly "legal." For example, the meaning of "gold-tranche purchases," never anchored in the original provisions, has changed in recent years, largely to accommodate purchases under the compensatory financing facility for developing countries. The amendment now provides a definition (Article XIX) and makes gold-tranche purchases, which thus far have enjoyed *"de facto* automaticity,"* legally automatic (Article V, Section 3). It will also remove the present limitation on making gold-tranche purchases for meeting capital transfers (Article VI, Sections 1 and 2). Finally, there are numerous changes in the rules on "repurchase by a member of its currency held by the Fund" (Article V, Section 7). A concept of gross monetary reserves is introduced as the basis of the calculations of members' repurchase obligations (Article XIX and Schedule B) and for certain other purposes.

Several modifications of the original Articles are not mentioned in this brief description. They would be relevant for a discussion of the operations of the General Account of the Fund, but have little or no bearing on the subjects of this essay, which relate chiefly to the new facility.

134

Appendix D

Proposed Additions to the Articles of Agreement

The following twelve Articles, numbered XXI to XXXII, and four Schedules, lettered F to I, are to be added to the Articles of Agreement of the International Monetary Fund:

Article XXI

Special Drawing Rights

Section 1. *Authority to allocate special drawing rights*

To meet the need, as and when it arises, for a supplement to existing reserve assets, the Fund is authorized to allocate special drawing rights to members that are participants in the Special Drawing Account.

Section 2. *Unit of value*

The unit of value of special drawing rights shall be equivalent to 0.888671 gram of fine gold.

Article XXII

General Account and Special Drawing Account

Section 1. *Separation of operations and transactions*

All operations and transactions involving special drawing rights shall be conducted through the Special Drawing Account. All other operations and transactions of the Fund authorized by or under this Agreement shall be conducted through the General Account. Operations and transactions pursuant to Article XXIII, Section 2, shall be conducted through the General Account as well as the Special Drawing Account.

Section 2. *Separation of assets and property*

All assets and property of the Fund shall be held in the General Account, except that assets and property acquired under Article XXVI, Section 2, and Articles XXX and XXXI and Schedules H and I shall be held in the Special Drawing Account. Any assets or property held in one Account shall not be available to discharge or meet the liabilities, obligations, or losses of the Fund incurred in the conduct of the operations and transactions of the other Account, except that the expenses of conducting the business of the Special Drawing Account shall be paid by the Fund from the General Account which shall be reimbursed from time to time by assessments under Article XXVI, Section 4, made on the basis of a reasonable estimate of such expenses.

Section 3. *Recording and information*

All changes in holdings of special drawing rights shall take effect only when recorded by the Fund in the Special Drawing Account. Participants shall notify the Fund of the provisions of this Agreement under which special drawing rights are used. The Fund may require participants to furnish it with such other information as it deems necessary for its functions.

Article XXIII

Participants and Other Holders of Special Drawing Rights

Section 1. *Participants*

Each member of the Fund that deposits with the Fund an instrument setting forth that it undertakes all the obligations of a participant in the Special Drawing Account in accordance with its law and that it has taken all steps necessary to enable it to carry out all of these obligations shall become a participant in the Special Drawing Account as of the date the instrument is deposited, except that no member shall become a participant before Articles XXI through XXXII and Schedules F through I have entered into force and instruments have been deposited under this Section by members that have at least seventy-five percent of the total of quotas.

Section 2. *General Account as a holder*

The Fund may accept and hold special drawing rights in the General Account and use them, in accordance with the provisions of this Agreement.

Section 3. *Other holders*

The Fund by an eighty-five percent majority of the total voting power may prescribe:

(i) as holders, non-members, members that are non-participants, and institutions that perform functions of a central bank for more than one member;

(ii) the terms and conditions on which these holders may be permitted to accept, hold, and use special drawing rights, in operations and transactions with participants; and

(iii) the terms and conditions on which participants may enter into operations and transactions with these holders.

The terms and conditions prescribed by the Fund for the use of special drawing rights by prescribed holders and by participants in operations and transactions with them shall be consistent with the provisions of this Agreement.

Article XXIV

Allocation and Cancellation of Special Drawing Rights

Section 1. *Principles and considerations governing allocation and cancellation*

(a) In all its decisions with respect to the allocation and cancellation of special drawing rights the Fund shall seek to meet the long-term global need, as and when it arises, to supplement existing reserve assets in such manner as will promote the attainment of its purposes and will avoid economic stagnation and deflation as well as excess demand and inflation in the world.

(b) The first decision to allocate special drawing rights shall take into account, as special considerations, a collective judgment that there is a global need to supplement reserves, and the attainment of a better balance of payments equilibrium, as well as the likelihood of a better working of the adjustment process in the future.

Section 2. *Allocation and cancellation*

(a) Decisions of the Fund to allocate or cancel special drawing rights shall be made for basic periods which shall run consecutively and shall be five years in duration. The first basic period shall begin on the date of the first decision to allocate special drawing rights or such later date as may be specified in that decision. Any allocations or cancellations shall take place at yearly intervals.

(b) The rates at which allocations are to be made shall be expressed as percentages of quotas on the date of each decision to allocate. The rates at which special drawing rights are to be cancelled shall be expressed as percentages of net cumulative allocations of special drawing rights on the date of each decision to cancel. The percentages shall be the same for all participants.

(c) In its decision for any basic period the Fund may provide, notwithstanding (a) and (b) above, that:

(i) the duration of the basic period shall be other than five years; or

(ii) the allocations or cancellations shall take place at other than yearly intervals; or

(iii) the basis for allocations or cancellations shall be the quotas or net cumulative allocations on dates other than the dates of decisions to allocate or cancel.

(d) A member that becomes a participant after a basic period starts shall receive allocations beginning with the next basic period in which allocations are made after it becomes a participant unless the Fund decides that the new participant shall start to receive allocations beginning with the next allocation after it becomes a participant. If the Fund decides that a member that becomes a participant during a basic period shall receive allocations during the remainder of that basic period and the participant was not a member on the dates established under (b) or (c) above, the Fund shall determine the basis on which these allocations to the participant shall be made.

(e) A participant shall receive allocations of special drawing rights made pursuant to any decision to allocate unless:

(i) the governor for the participant did not vote in favor of the decision; and

(ii) the participant has notified the Fund in writing prior to the first allocation of special drawing rights under that decision that it does not wish special drawing rights to be allocated to it under the decision.

On the request of a participant, the Fund may decide to terminate the effect of the notice with respect to allocations of special drawing rights subsequent to the termination.

(f) If on the effective date of any cancellation the amount of special drawing rights held by a participant is less than its share of the special drawing rights that are to be cancelled, the participant shall eliminate its negative balance as promptly as its gross reserve position permits and shall remain in consultation with the Fund for this purpose. Special drawing rights acquired by the participant after the effective date of the cancellation shall be applied against its negative balance and cancelled.

Section 3. *Unexpected major developments*

The Fund may change the rates or intervals of allocation or cancellation during the rest of a basic period or change the length of a basic period or start a new basic period, if at any time the Fund finds it desirable to do so because of unexpected major developments.

Section 4. *Decisions on allocations and cancellations*

(a) Decisions under Section 2(a), (b), and (c) or Section 3 of this Article shall be made by the Board of Governors on the basis of proposals of the Managing Director concurred in by the Executive Directors.

(b) Before making any proposal, the Managing Director, after having satisfied himself that it will be consistent with the provisions of Section 1(a) of this Article, shall conduct such consultations as will enable him to ascertain that there is broad support among participants for the proposal. In addition, before making a proposal for the first allocation, the Managing Director shall satisfy himself that the provisions of Section 1(b) of this Article have been met and that there is broad support among participants to begin allocations; he shall make a proposal for the first allocation as soon after the establishment of the Special Drawing Account as he is so satisfied.

(c) The Managing Director shall make proposals:

(i) not later than six months before the end of each basic period;

(ii) if no decision has been taken with respect to allocation or cancellation for a basic period, whenever he is satisfied that the provisions of (b) above have been met;

(iii) when, in accordance with Section 3 of this Article, he considers that it would be desirable to change the rate or intervals of allocation or cancellation or change the length of a basic period or start a new basic period; or

(iv) within six months of a request by the Board of Governors or the Executive Directors;

provided that, if under (i), (iii), or (iv) above the Managing Director ascertains that there is no proposal which he considers to be consistent with the provisions of Section 1 of this Article that has broad support among participants in accordance with (b) above, he shall report to the Board of Governors and to the Executive Directors.

(d) A majority of eighty-five percent of the total voting power shall be required for decisions under Section 2(a), (b), and (c) or Section 3 of this Article except for decisions under Section 3 with respect to a decrease in the rates of allocation.

Article XXV

Operations and Transactions in Special Drawing Rights

Section 1. *Use of special drawing rights*

Special drawing rights may be used in the operations and transactions authorized by or under this Agreement.

Section 2. *Transactions between participants*

(a) A participant shall be entitled to use its special drawing rights to obtain an equivalent amount of currency from a participant designated under Section 5 of this Article.

(b) A participant, in agreement with another participant, may use its special drawing rights:

(i) to obtain an equivalent amount of its own currency held by the other participant; or

(ii) to obtain an equivalent amount of currency from the other participant in any transactions, prescribed by the Fund, that would promote reconstitution by the other participant under Section 6(a) of this Article; prevent or reduce a negative balance of the other participant; offset the effect of a failure by the other participant to fulfill the expectation in Section 3(a) of this Article; or bring the holdings of special drawing rights by both participants closer to their net cumulative allocations. The Fund by an eighty-five percent majority of the total voting power may prescribe additional transactions or categories of transactions under this provision. Any transactions or categories of transactions prescribed by the Fund under this subsection (b)(ii) shall be consistent with the other provisions of this Agreement and with the proper use of special drawing rights in accordance with this Agreement.

(c) A participant that provides currency to a participant using special drawing rights shall receive an equivalent amount of special drawing rights.

Section 3. *Requirement of need*

(a) In transactions under Section 2 of this Article, except as otherwise provided in (c) below, a participant will be expected to use its special drawing rights only to meet balance of payments needs or in the light of developments in its official holdings of gold, foreign exchange, and special drawing rights, and its reserve position in the Fund, and not for the sole purpose of changing the composition of the foregoing as between special drawing rights and the total of gold, foreign exchange, and reserve position in the Fund.

(b) The use of special drawing rights shall not be subject to challenge on the basis of the expectation in (a) above, but the Fund may make representations to a participant that fails to fulfill this expectation. A participant that persists in failing to fulfill this expectation shall be subject to Article XXIX, Section 2(b).

(c) Participants may use special drawing rights without fulfilling the expectation in (a) above to obtain an equivalent amount of currency from another participant in any transactions, prescribed by the Fund, that would promote reconstitution by the other participant under Section 6(a) of this Article; prevent or reduce a negative balance of the other participant; offset the effect of a failure by the other participant to fulfill the expectation in (a) above; or bring the holdings of special drawing rights by both participants closer to their net cumulative allocations.

Section 4. *Obligation to provide currency*

A participant designated by the Fund under Section 5 of this Article shall provide on demand currency convertible in fact to a participant using special drawing rights under Section 2(a) of this Article. A participant's obligation to provide currency shall not extend beyond the point at which its holdings of special drawing rights in excess of its net cumulative allocation are equal to twice its net cumulative allocation or such higher limit as may be agreed between a participant and the Fund. A participant may provide currency in excess of the obligatory limit or any agreed higher limit.

Section 5. *Designation of participants to provide currency*

(a) The Fund shall ensure that a participant will be able to use its special drawing rights by designating participants to provide currency for specified amounts of special drawing rights for the purposes of Sections 2(a) and 4 of this Article. Designations shall be made in accordance with the following general principles supplemented by such other principles as the Fund may adopt from time to time:

(i) A participant shall be subject to designation if its balance of payments and gross reserve position is sufficiently strong, but this will not preclude the possibility that a participant with a strong reserve position will be designated even though it has a moderate balance of payments deficit. Participants shall be designated in such manner as will promote over time a balanced distribution of holdings of special drawing rights among them.

(ii) Participants shall be subject to designation in order to promote reconstitution under Section 6(a) of this Article; to reduce negative balances in holdings of special drawing rights; or to offset the effect of failures to fulfill the expectation in Section 3(a) of this Article.

(iii) In designating participants the Fund normally shall give priority to those that need to acquire special drawing rights to meet the objectives of designation under (ii) above.

(b) In order to promote over time a balanced distribution of holdings of special drawing rights under (a)(i) above, the Fund shall apply the rules for designation in Schedule F or such rules as may be adopted under (c) below.

(c) The rules for designation shall be reviewed before the end of the first and each subsequent basic period and the Fund may adopt new rules as the result of a review. Unless new rules are adopted, the rules in force at the time of the review shall continue to apply.

Section 6. *Reconstitution*

(a) Participants that use their special drawing rights shall reconstitute their holdings of them in accordance with the rules for reconstitution in Schedule G or such rules as may be adopted under (b) below.

(b) The rules for reconstitution shall be reviewed before the end of the first and each subsequent basic period and new rules shall be adopted if necessary. Unless new rules are adopted or a decision is made to abrogate rules for reconstitution, the rules in force at the time of the review shall continue to apply. An eighty-five percent majority of the total voting power shall be required for decisions to adopt, modify, or abrogate the rules for reconstitution.

Section 7. *Operations and transactions through the General Account*

(a) Special drawing rights shall be included in a member's monetary reserves under Article XIX for the purposes of Article III, Section 4(a), Article V, Section 7(b) and (c), Article V, Section 8(f), and Schedule B, paragraph 1. The Fund may decide that in calculating monetary reserves and the increase in monetary reserves during any year for the purpose of Article V, Section 7(b) and (c), no account shall be taken of any increase or decrease in those monetary reserves which is due to allocations or cancellations of special drawing rights during the year.

(b) The Fund shall accept special drawing rights:

(i) in repurchases accruing in special drawing rights under Article V, Section 7(b); and

(ii) in reimbursement pursuant to Article XXVI, Section 4.

(c) The Fund may accept special drawing rights to the extent it may decide:

(i) in payment of charges; and

(ii) in repurchases other than those under Article V, Section 7(b), in proportions which, as far as feasible, shall be the same for all members.

(d) The Fund, if it deems such action appropriate to replenish its holdings of a participant's currency and after consultation with that participant on alternative ways of replenishment under Article VII, Section 2, may require that participant to provide its currency for special drawing rights held in the General Account subject to Section 4 of this Article. In replenishing with special drawing rights, the Fund shall pay due regard to the principles of designation under Section 5 of this Article.

(e) To the extent that a participant may receive special drawing rights in a transaction prescribed by the Fund to promote reconstitution by it under

Section 6(a) of this Article, prevent or reduce a negative balance, or offset the effect of a failure by it to fulfill the expectation in Section 3(a) of this Article, the Fund may provide the participant with special drawing rights held in the General Account for gold or currency acceptable to the Fund.

(f) In any of the other operations and transactions of the Fund with a participant conducted through the General Account the Fund may use special drawing rights by agreement with the participant.

(g) The Fund may levy reasonable charges uniform for all participants in connection with operations and transactions under this Section.

Section 8.   *Exchange rates*

(a) The exchange rates for operations or transactions between participants shall be such that a participant using special drawing rights shall receive the same value whatever currencies might be provided and whichever participants provide those currencies, and the Fund shall adopt regulations to give effect to this principle.

(b) The Fund shall consult a participant on the procedure for determining rates of exchange for its currency.

(c) For the purpose of this provision the term participant includes a terminating participant.

Article XXVI

Special Drawing Account
Interest and Charges

Section 1.   *Interest*

Interest at the same rate for all holders shall be paid by the Fund to each holder on the amount of its holdings of special drawing rights. The Fund shall pay the amount due to each holder whether or not sufficient charges are received to meet the payment of interest.

Section 2.   *Charges*

Charges at the same rate for all participants shall be paid to the Fund by each participant on the amount of its net cumulative allocation of special drawing rights plus any negative balance of the participant or unpaid charges.

Section 3.   *Rate of interest and charges*

The rate of interest shall be equal to the rate of charges and shall be one and one-half percent per annum. The Fund in its discretion may increase or reduce this rate, but the rate shall not be greater than two percent or the rate of remuneration decided under Article V, Section 9, whichever is higher, or smaller than one percent or the rate of remuneration decided under Article V, Section 9, whichever is lower.

Section 4.   *Assessments*

When it is decided under Article XXII, Section 2, that reimbursements shall be made, the Fund shall levy assessments for this purpose at the same rate for all participants on their net cumulative allocations.

Section 5. *Payment of interest, charges, and assessments*

Interest, charges, and assessments shall be paid in special drawing rights. A participant that needs special drawing rights to pay any charge or assessment shall be obligated and entitled to obtain them, at its option for gold or currency acceptable to the Fund, in a transaction with the Fund conducted through the General Account. If sufficient special drawing rights cannot be obtained in this way, the participant shall be obligated and entitled to obtain them with currency convertible in fact from a participant which the Fund shall specify. Special drawing rights acquired by a participant after the date for payment shall be applied against its unpaid charges and cancelled.

Article XXVII

Administration of the General Account and the Special Drawing Account

(a) The General Account and the Special Drawing Account shall be administered in accordance with the provisions of Article XII, subject to the following:

(i) The Board of Governors may delegate to the Executive Directors authority to exercise any powers of the Board with respect to special drawing rights except those under Article XXIII, Section 3, Article XXIV, Section 2(a), (b), and (c), and Section 3, the penultimate sentence of Article XXV, Section 2(b), Article XXV, Section 6(b), and Article XXXI(a).

(ii) For meetings of or decisions by the Board of Governors on matters pertaining exclusively to the Special Drawing Account only requests by or the presence and the votes of governors appointed by members that are participants shall be counted for the purpose of calling meetings and determining whether a quorum exists or whether a decision is made by the required majority.

(iii) For decisions by the Executive Directors on matters pertaining exclusively to the Special Drawing Account only directors appointed or elected by at least one member that is a participant shall be entitled to vote. Each of these directors shall be entitled to cast the number of votes allotted to the member which is a participant that appointed him or to the members that are participants whose votes counted towards his election. Only the presence of directors appointed or elected by members that are participants and the votes allotted to members that are participants shall be counted for the purpose of determining whether a quorum exists or whether a decision is made by the required majority.

(iv) Questions of the general administration of the Fund, including reimbursement under Article XXII, Section 2, and any question whether a matter pertains to both Accounts or exclusively to the Special Drawing Account shall be decided as if they pertained exclusively to the General Account. Decisions with respect to the acceptance and holding of special drawing rights in the General Account and the use of them, and other decisions affecting the operations and transactions conducted through both the General Account and the Special Drawing Account shall be made by the majorities required for decisions on matters pertaining exclusively to each Account. A decision on a matter pertaining to the Special Drawing Account shall so indicate.

(b) In addition to the privileges and immunities that are accorded under Article IX of this Agreement, no tax of any kind shall be levied on special drawing rights or on operations or transactions in special drawing rights.

(c) A question of interpretation of the provisions of this Agreement on matters pertaining exclusively to the Special Drawing Account shall be submitted to the Executive Directors pursuant to Article XVIII(a) only on the request of a participant. In any case where the Executive Directors have given a decision on a question of interpretation pertaining exclusively to the Special Drawing Account only a participant may require that the question be referred to the Board of Governors under Article XVIII(b). The Board of Governors shall decide whether a governor appointed by a member that is not a participant shall be entitled to vote in the Committee on Interpretation on questions pertaining exclusively to the Special Drawing Account.

(d) Whenever a disagreement arises between the Fund and a participant that has terminated its participation in the Special Drawing Account or between the Fund and any participant during the liquidation of the Special Drawing Account with respect to any matter arising exclusively from participation in the Special Drawing Account, the disagreement shall be submitted to arbitration in accordance with the procedures in Article XVIII(c).

Article XXVIII

General Obligations of Participants

In addition to the obligations assumed with respect to special drawing rights under other Articles of this Agreement, each participant undertakes to collaborate with the Fund and with other participants in order to facilitate the effective functioning of the Special Drawing Account and the proper use of special drawing rights in accordance with this Agreement.

Article XXIX

Suspension of Transactions in Special Drawing Rights

Section 1.   *Emergency provisions*

In the event of an emergency or the development of unforeseen circumstances threatening the operations of the Fund with respect to the Special Drawing Account, the Executive Directors by unanimous vote may suspend for a period of not more than one hundred twenty days the operation of any of the provisions relating to special drawing rights, and the provisions of Article XVI, Section 1(b), (c), and (d), shall then apply.

Section 2. *Failure to fulfill obligations*

(a) If the Fund finds that a participant has failed to fulfill its obligations under Article XXV, Section 4, the right of the participant to use its special drawing rights shall be suspended unless the Fund otherwise determines.

(b) If the Fund finds that a participant has failed to fulfill any other obligation with respect to special drawing rights, the Fund may suspend the right of the participant to use special drawing rights it acquires after the suspension.

(c) Regulations shall be adopted to ensure that before action is taken against any participant under (a) or (b) above, the participant shall be informed immediately of the complaint against it and given an adequate opportunity for stating its case, both orally and in writing. Whenever the participant is thus informed of a complaint relating to (a) above, it shall not use special drawing rights pending the disposition of the complaint.

(d) Suspension under (a) or (b) above or limitation under (c) above shall not affect a participant's obligation to provide currency in accordance with Article XXV, Section 4.

(e) The Fund may at any time terminate a suspension under (a) or (b) above, provided that a suspension imposed on a participant under (b) above for failure to fulfill the obligation under Article XXV, Section 6(a), shall not be terminated until one hundred eighty days after the end of the first calendar quarter during which the participant complies with the rules for reconstitution.

(f) The right of a participant to use its special drawing rights shall not be suspended because it has become ineligible to use the Fund's resources under Article IV, Section 6, Article V, Section 5, Article VI, Section 1, or Article XV, Section 2(a). Article XV, Section 2, shall not apply because a participant has failed to fulfill any obligations with respect to special drawing rights.

Article XXX

Termination of Participation

Section 1. *Right to terminate participation*

(a) Any participant may terminate its participation in the Special Drawing Account at any time by transmitting a notice in writing to the Fund at its principal office. Termination shall become effective on the date the notice is received.

(b) A participant that withdraws from membership in the Fund shall be deemed to have simultaneously terminated its participation in the Special Drawing Account.

Section 2. *Settlement on termination*

(a) When a participant terminates its participation in the Special Drawing Account, all operations and transactions by the terminating participant in special drawing rights shall cease except as otherwise permitted under an agreement made pursuant to (c) below in order to facilitate a settlement or as provided in Sections 3, 5, and 6 of this Article or in Schedule H. Interest and charges that accrued to the date of termination and assessments levied before that date but not paid shall be paid in special drawing rights.

(b) The Fund shall be obligated to redeem all special drawing rights held by the terminating participant, and the terminating participant shall be obligated to pay to the Fund an amount equal to its net cumulative allocation and any other amounts that may be due and payable because of its participation in the Special Drawing Account. These obligations shall be set off against each other and the amount of special drawing rights held by the terminating participant that is used in the setoff to extinguish its obligation to the Fund shall be cancelled.

(c) A settlement shall be made with reasonable dispatch by agreement between the terminating participant and the Fund with respect to any obligation of the terminating participant or the Fund after the setoff in (b) above. If agreement on a settlement is not reached promptly the provisions of Schedule H shall apply.

Section 3.   *Interest and charges*

After the date of termination the Fund shall pay interest on any outstanding balance of special drawing rights held by a terminating participant and the terminating participant shall pay charges on any outstanding obligation owed to the Fund at the times and rates prescribed under Article XXVI. Payment shall be made in special drawing rights. A terminating participant shall be entitled to obtain special drawing rights with currency convertible in fact to pay charges or assessments in a transaction with a participant specified by the Fund or by agreement from any other holder, or to dispose of special drawing rights received as interest in a transaction with any participant designated under Article XXV, Section 5, or by agreement with any other holder.

Section 4.   *Settlement of obligation to the Fund*

Gold or currency received by the Fund from a terminating participant shall be used by the Fund to redeem special drawing rights held by participants in proportion to the amount by which each participant's holdings of special drawing rights exceed its net cumulative allocation at the time the gold or currency is received by the Fund. Special drawing rights so redeemed and special drawing rights obtained by a terminating participant under the provisions of this Agreement to meet any installment due under an agreement on settlement or under Schedule H and set off against that installment shall be cancelled.

Section 5.   *Settlement of obligation to a terminating participant*

Whenever the Fund is required to redeem special drawing rights held by a terminating participant, redemption shall be made with currency or gold provided by participants specified by the Fund. These participants shall be specified in accordance with the principles in Article XXV, Section 5. Each specified participant shall provide at its option the currency of the terminating participant or currency convertible in fact or gold to the Fund and shall receive an equivalent amount of special drawing rights. However, a terminating participant may use its special drawing rights to obtain its own currency, currency convertible in fact, or gold from any holder, if the Fund so permits.

Section 6. *General Account transactions*

In order to facilitate settlement with a terminating participant the Fund may decide that a terminating participant shall:

> (i) use any special drawing rights held by it after the setoff in Section 2(b) of this Article, when they are to be redeemed, in a transaction with the Fund conducted through the General Account to obtain its own currency or currency convertible in fact at the option of the Fund; or
>
> (ii) obtain special drawing rights in a transaction with the Fund conducted through the General Account for a currency acceptable to the Fund or gold to meet any charges or installment due under an agreement or the provisions of Schedule H.

Article XXXI
Liquidation of the Special Drawing Account

(a) The Special Drawing Account may not be liquidated except by decision of the Board of Governors. In an emergency, if the Executive Directors decide that liquidation of the Special Drawing Account may be necessary, they may temporarily suspend allocations or cancellations and all transactions in special drawing rights pending decision by the Board. A decision by the Board of Governors to liquidate the Fund shall be a decision to liquidate both the General Account and the Special Drawing Account.

(b) If the Board of Governors decides to liquidate the Special Drawing Account, all allocations or cancellations and all operations and transactions in special drawing rights and the activities of the Fund with respect to the Special Drawing Account shall cease except those incidental to the orderly discharge of the obligations of participants and of the Fund with respect to special drawing rights, and all obligations of the Fund and of participants under this Agreement with respect to special drawing rights shall cease except those set out in this Article, Article XVIII(c), Article XXVI, Article XXVII(d), Article XXX and Schedule H, or any agreement reached under Article XXX subject to paragraph 4 of Schedule H, Article XXXII, and Schedule I.

(c) Upon liquidation of the Special Drawing Account, interest and charges that accrued to the date of liquidation and assessments levied before that date but not paid shall be paid in special drawing rights. The Fund shall be obligated to redeem all special drawing rights held by holders and each participant shall be obligated to pay the Fund an amount equal to its net cumulative allocation of special drawing rights and such other amounts as may be due and payable because of its participation in the Special Drawing Account.

(d) Liquidation of the Special Drawing Account shall be administered in accordance with the provisions of Schedule I.

Article XXXII

Explanation of Terms With Respect to
Special Drawing Rights

In interpreting the provisions of this Agreement with respect to special drawing rights the Fund and its members shall be guided by the following:

(a) Net cumulative allocation of special drawing rights means the total amount of special drawing rights allocated to a participant less its share of special drawing rights that have been cancelled under Article XXIV, Section 2(a).

(b) Currency convertible in fact means:

(1) a participant's currency for which a procedure exists for the conversion of balances of the currency obtained in transactions involving special drawing rights into each other currency for which such procedure exists, at rates of exchange prescribed under Article XXV, Section 8, and which is the currency of a participant that

(i) has accepted the obligations of Article VIII, Sections 2, 3, and 4, or

(ii) for the settlement of international transactions in fact freely buys and sells gold within the limits prescribed by the Fund under Section 2 of Article IV; or

(2) currency convertible into a currency described in paragraph (1) above at rates of exchange prescribed under Article XXV, Section 8.

(c) A participant's reserve position in the Fund means the sum of the gold tranche purchases it could make and the amount of any indebtedness of the Fund which is readily repayable to the participant under a loan agreement.

Schedule F

Designation

During the first basic period the rules for designation shall be as follows:

(a) Participants subject to designation under Article XXV, Section 5(a)(i), shall be designated for such amounts as will promote over time equality in the ratios of the participants' holdings of special drawing rights in excess of their net cumulative allocations to their official holdings of gold and foreign exchange.

(b) The formula to give effect to (a) above shall be such that participants subject to designation shall be designated:

(i) in proportion to their official holdings of gold and foreign exchange when the ratios described in (a) above are equal; and

(ii) in such manner as gradually to reduce the difference between the ratios described in (a) above that are low and the ratios that are high.

Schedule G

Reconstitution

1. During the first basic period the rules for reconstitution shall be as follows:

(a) (i) A participant shall so use and reconstitute its holdings of special drawing rights that, five years after the first allocation and at the end of each calendar quarter thereafter, the average of its total daily holdings of special drawing rights over the most recent five-year period will be not less than thirty percent of the average of its daily net cumulative allocation of special drawing rights over the same period.

(ii) Two years after the first allocation and at the end of each calendar month thereafter the Fund shall make calculations for each participant so as to ascertain whether and to what extent the participant would need to acquire special drawing rights between the date of the calculation and the end of any five-year period in order to comply with the requirement in (a)(i) above. The Fund shall adopt regulations with respect to the bases on which these calculations shall be made and with respect to the timing of the designation of participants under Article XXV, Section 5(a)(ii), in order to assist them to comply with the requirement in (a)(i) above.

(iii) The Fund shall give special notice to a participant when the calculations under (a)(ii) above indicate that it is unlikely that the participant will be able to comply with the requirement in (a)(i) above unless it ceases to use special drawing rights for the rest of the period for which the calculation was made under (a)(ii) above.

(iv) A participant that needs to acquire special drawing rights to fulfill this obligation shall be obligated and entitled to obtain them, at its option for gold or currency acceptable to the Fund, in a transaction with the Fund conducted through the General Account. If sufficient special drawing rights to fulfill this obligation cannot be obtained in this way, the participant shall be obligated and entitled to obtain them with currency convertible in fact from a participant which the Fund shall specify.

(b) Participants shall also pay due regard to the desirability of pursuing over time a balanced relationship between their holdings of special drawing rights and their holdings of gold and foreign exchange and their reserve positions in the Fund.

2. If a participant fails to comply with the rules for reconstitution, the Fund shall determine whether or not the circumstances justify suspension under Article XXIX, Section 2(b).

Schedule H

Termination of Participation

1. If the obligation remaining after the setoff under Article XXX, Section 2(b), is to the terminating participant and agreement on settlement between the Fund and the terminating participant is not reached within six months of the date of termination, the Fund shall redeem this balance of special drawing rights in equal half-yearly installments within a maximum of five years of the date of termination. The Fund shall redeem this balance as it may determine, either (a) by the payment to the terminating participant of the amounts provided by the remaining participants to the Fund in accordance with Article XXX, Section 5, or (b) by permitting the terminating participant to use its special drawing rights to obtain its own currency or currency convertible in fact from a participant specified by the Fund, the General Account, or any other holder.

2. If the obligation remaining after the setoff under Article XXX, Section 2(b), is to the Fund and agreement on settlement is not reached within six months of the date of termination, the terminating participant shall discharge this obligation in equal half-yearly installments within three years of the date of termination or within such longer period as may be fixed by the Fund. The terminating participant shall discharge this obligation, as the Fund may determine, either (a) by the payment to the Fund of currency convertible in fact or gold at the option of the terminating participant, or (b) by obtaining special drawing rights, in accordance with Article XXX, Section 6, from the General Account or in agreement with a participant specified by the Fund or from any other holder, and the setoff of these special drawing rights against the installment due.

3. Installments under either 1 or 2 above shall fall due six months after the date of termination and at intervals of six months thereafter.

4. In the event of the Special Drawing Account going into liquidation under Article XXXI within six months of the date a participant terminates its participation, the settlement between the Fund and that government shall be made in accordance with Article XXXI and Schedule I.

Schedule I

Administration of Liquidation of the
Special Drawing Account

1. In the event of liquidation of the Special Drawing Account, participants shall discharge their obligations to the Fund in ten half-yearly installments, or in such longer period as the Fund may decide is needed, in currency convertible in fact and the currencies of participants holding special drawing rights to be redeemed in any installment to the extent of such redemption, as determined by the Fund. The first half-yearly payment shall be made six months after the decision to liquidate the Special Drawing Account.

2. If it is decided to liquidate the Fund within six months of the date of the decision to liquidate the Special Drawing Account, the liquidation of the Special Drawing Account shall not proceed until special drawing rights held in the General Account have been distributed in accordance with the following rule:

> After the distribution made under 2(a) of Schedule E, the Fund shall apportion its special drawing rights held in the General Account among all members that are participants in proportion to the amounts due to each participant after the distribution under 2(a). To determine the amount due to each member for the purpose of apportioning the remainder of its holdings of each currency under 2(c) of Schedule E, the Fund shall deduct the distribution of special drawing rights made under this rule.

3. With the amounts received under 1 above, the Fund shall redeem special drawing rights held by holders in the following manner and order:

(a) Special drawing rights held by governments that have terminated their participation more than six months before the date the Board of Governors decides to liquidate the Special Drawing Account shall be redeemed in accordance with the terms of any agreement under Article XXX or Schedule H.

(b) Special drawing rights held by holders that are not participants shall be redeemed before those held by participants, and shall be redeemed in proportion to the amount held by each holder.

(c) The Fund shall determine the proportion of special drawing rights held by each participant in relation to its net cumulative allocation. The Fund shall first redeem special drawing rights from the participants with the highest proportion until this proportion is reduced to that of the second highest proportion; the Fund shall then redeem the special drawing rights held by these participants in accordance with their net cumulative allocations until the proportions are reduced to that of the third highest proportion; and this process shall be continued until the amount available for redemption is exhausted.

4. Any amount that a participant will be entitled to receive in redemption under 3 above shall be set off against any amount to be paid under 1 above.

5. During liquidation the Fund shall pay interest on the amount of special drawing rights held by holders, and each participant shall pay charges on the net cumulative allocation of special drawing rights to it less the amount of any payments made in accordance with 1 above. The rates of interest and charges and the time of payment shall be determined by the Fund. Payments of interest and charges shall be made in special drawing rights to the extent possible. A participant that does not hold sufficient special drawing rights to meet any charges shall make the payment with gold or a currency specified by the Fund. Special drawing rights received as charges in amounts needed for administrative expenses shall not be used for the payment of interest, but shall be transferred to the Fund and shall be redeemed first and with the currencies used by the Fund to meet its expenses.

6. While a participant is in default with respect to any payment required by 1 or 5 above, no amounts shall be paid to it in accordance with 2 or 5 above.

7. If after the final payments have been made to participants each participant not in default does not hold special drawing rights in the same proportion to its net cumulative allocation, those participants holding a lower proportion shall purchase from those holding a higher proportion such amounts in accordance with arrangements made by the Fund as will make the proportion of their holdings of special drawing rights the same. Each participant in default shall pay to the Fund its own currency in an amount equal to its default. The Fund shall apportion this currency and any residual claims among participants in proportion to the amount of special drawing rights held by each and these special drawing rights shall be cancelled. The Fund shall then close the books of the Special Drawing Account and all of the Fund's liabilities arising from the allocations of special drawing rights and the administration of the Special Drawing Account shall cease.

8. Each participant whose currency is distributed to other participants under this Schedule guarantees the unrestricted use of such currency at all times for the purchase of goods or for payments of sums due to it or to persons in its territories. Each participant so obligated agrees to compensate other participants for any loss resulting from the difference between the value at which the Fund distributed its currency under this Schedule and the value realized by such participants on disposal of its currency.

Appendix E

IMPACT OF HYPOTHETICAL ALLOCATION OF SDR'S ON THE BALANCES OF PAYMENTS OF FUND MEMBER COUNTRIES

(in millions of dollars)

COUNTRY	OFFICIAL BALANCE OF PAYMENTS				IMF QUOTA DEC. 1966	ALLOCATION OF SDR'S 10% OF QUOTA	CORRECTED BALANCE OF PAYMENTS			
	1965		1966				1965		1966	
	SURPLUS	DEFICIT	SURPLUS	DEFICIT			SURPLUS	DEFICIT	SURPLUS	DEFICIT
I. The Ten										
Belgium-Luxembourg	162		31		422	42.2	205.8		74.8	
					16	1.6				
France	711		393		985	98.5	809.5		491.5	
Germany		494	581		1,200	120.0		374.0	701.0	
Italy	957		169		625	62.5	1,019.5		231.5	
Netherlands	72		42		520	52.0	124.0		94.0	
Subtotal: The Five	**1,902**	**494**	**1,216**		**3,768**	**376.8**	**2,158.8**	**374.0**	**1,592.8**	
Sweden	2		56		225	22.5	24.5		78.5	
Canada	146			332	740	74.0	220.0			258.0
Japan	120			54	725	72.5	192.5		18.5	
Subtotal: The Eight	**2,170**	**494**	**1,272**	**386**	**5,458**	**545.8**	**2,595.8**	**374.0**	**1,689.8**	**258.0**
United Kingdom		344		1,567	2,440	244.0		100.0		1,323.0
United States		1,304	225		5,160	516.0		788.0	741.0	
Subtotal: The Ten	**2,170**	**2,142**	**1,467**	**1,953**	**13,058**	**1,305.8**	**2,595.8**	**1,262.0**	**2,430.8**	**1,581.0**

II. Other Developed

Australia		358	50		500	50.0		308.0	100.0	
Austria		7	19		175	17.5		42.7	36.5	
Denmark		59	9		163	16.3	10.5	51.5	25.3	
Finland		64		126	125	12.5		23.0		113.5
Greece		33	23		100	10.0			33.0	
Iceland	6		4		15	1.5			5.5	
Ireland		36			80	8.0	7.5	28.0	91.0	
New Zealand		100	83	63	157	15.7		84.3		47.3
Norway	639		374		150	15.0	654.0		389.0	
Portugal	44		130		75	7.5	51.5		137.5	
South Africa		155	195		200	20.0		135.0	215.0	
Spain		123		182	250	25.0		98.0		157.0
Turkey	75				86	8.6	83.6	0	2.6	
Yugoslavia		15	44	6	150	15.0	0		59.0	
Subtotal: Other Developed – 14	**764**	**950**	**931**	**377**	**2,226**	**222.6**	**807.1**	**770.5**	**1,094.4**	**317.8**

III. Less Developed

(a) LATIN AMERICA

Argentina	180		104		35.0	350	215.0		139.0	
Bolivia	13		3		2.9	29	15.9		5.9	
Brazil	458		222		35.0	350	493.0		257.0	
Chile	39		66		10.0	100	49.0		76.0	
Colombia	66				12.5	125	78.5			39.5
Costa Rica		5		52	2.5	25				2.5
Dominican Republic				5	2.6	26		2.5		17.4
Ecuador	8	13	11	20	2.5	25	10.6	10.5	13.5	
El Salvador		1		15	2.5	25	1.5			12.5
Guatemala		1		8	2.5	25	1.5			5.5
Guiana	n.a.				1.5	15			n.a.	
Haiti		n.a.	0	0	1.5	15		.5		
Honduras	5	2	4		1.9	19	6.9		1.5	
Jamaica	0	0	9		3.0	30	3.0		5.9	
Mexico	20	58	1		27.0	270	21.9		12.0	
Nicaragua			3	11	1.9	19		31.0	28.0	
Panama		5		1	1.1	11		3.9	4.9	
Paraguay	7				1.5	15	8.5			9.9
Peru	14	1		22	4.7	47	18.7		.5	
Trinidad & Tobago				2	2.5	25	1.5			17.3
Uruguay			19		3.0	30	10.0		.5	
Venezuela	7	22		26	25.0	250	3.0		22.0	1.0
Subtotal: Latin America – 22	**817**	**108**	**442**	**162**	**1,826**	**182.6**	**938.5**	**48.4**	**566.7**	**105.6**

COUNTRY	OFFICIAL BALANCE OF PAYMENTS 1965 SURPLUS	1965 DEFICIT	1966 SURPLUS	1966 DEFICIT	IMF QUOTA DEC. 1966	ALLOCATION OF SDR's 10% OF QUOTA	CORRECTED BALANCE OF PAYMENTS 1965 SURPLUS	1965 DEFICIT	1966 SURPLUS	1966 DEFICIT
(b) MIDDLE EAST										
Cyprus	21		17		15	1.5	22.5		18.5	
Iran	62		8		125	12.5	74.5		20.5	
Iraq		15	59		80	8.0		7.0	67.0	
Israel	94			19	80	8.0	102.0			11.0
Jordan	63		27		13	1.3	64.3		28.3	
Kuwait		44	67		50	5.0		39.0	72.0	
Lebanon	6		n.a.		7	.7	6.7		n.a.	
Saudi Arabia	123		76		90	9.0	132.0		85.0	
Syria		1		10	38	3.8	2.8			6.2
United Arab Rep.		73	3		150	15.0		58.0	18.0	
Subtotal: Middle East – 10	**369**	**133**	**257**	**29**	**648**	**64.8**	**404.8**	**104.0**	**309.3**	**17.2**
(c) OTHER ASIA										
Afghanistan		1		5	29	2.9	1.9			2.1
Burma		27	7		30	3.0		24.0	10.0	
Ceylon	34			53	78	7.8	41.8			45.2
China (Taiwan)[a]	8		22		550	55.0	63.0		77.0	
India		103		67	750	75.0		28.0	8.0	
Indonesia[b]	—		—		207	20.7	—		—	
Korea	4		118		24	2.4	6.4		120.4	
Laos	n.a.		n.a.		8	.8	n.a.		n.a.	
Malaysia	21			35	84	8.4	29.4			26.6
Nepal	10			14	10	1.0	11.0			13.0
Pakistan		67		9	188	18.8		48.2	9.8	
Philippines		15		17	110	11.0		4.0		6.0
Singapore	0		15		30	3.0	3.0		18.0	
Thailand	80		185		95	9.5	89.5		194.5	
Vietnam	37		128		24	2.4	39.4		130.4	
Subtotal: Other Asia – 15	**194**	**213**	**475**	**200**	**2,217**	**221.7**	**285.4**	**104.2**	**568.1**	**92.9**

(d) OTHER AFRICA

Algeria	16	n.a.		n.a.	63	6.3		n.a.	n.a.	n.a.
Burundi		n.a.		n.a.	15	1.5		n.a.	n.a.	n.a.
Cameroon		n.a.		n.a.	16	1.6		n.a.	n.a.	n.a.
Central African Republic		n.a.		n.a.	8	.8		n.a.	n.a.	n.a.
Chad		n.a.		n.a.	8	.8		n.a.	n.a.	n.a.
Congo (Brazzaville)		n.a.		n.a.	8	.8		n.a.	n.a.	n.a.
Congo (Dem. Rep.)		n.a.		n.a.	57	5.7		n.a.	n.a.	n.a.
Dahomey		n.a.	1	n.a.	8	.8		n.a.	n.a.	n.a.
Ethiopia					19	1.9	17.9	n.a.	2.9	
Gabon		73		n.a.	8	.8		66.1	n.a.	16.1
Ghana				23	69	6.9		n.a.	n.a.	n.a.
Guinea		n.a.		n.a.	19	1.9		n.a.	n.a.	n.a.
Ivory Coast	21		1		16	1.6	22.6		2.6	
Kenya	3		10		32	3.2	6.2		13.2	
Libya	76		94		19	1.9	77.9		95.9	
Liberia					20	2.0		n.a.	n.a.	n.a.
Malagasy Republic	12	n.a.		n.a.	11	1.1		n.a.	n.a.	n.a.
Malawi				5	11	1.1	13.1	2.3		3.9
Mali		4		2	17	1.7		n.a.		.3
Mauritania		n.a.		n.a.	8	.8		n.a.	n.a.	2.4
Morocco	51			10	76	7.6	58.6			n.a.
Niger		n.a.		n.a.	8	.8		n.a.	n.a.	21.7
Nigeria	14			28	63	6.3	20.3			n.a.
Rwanda					12	1.2		n.a.	n.a.	n.a.
Senegal		n.a.		n.a.	25	2.5		n.a.	n.a.	n.a.
Sierra Leone		3		6	15	1.5		1.5	1.5	4.5
Somalia		3	0	0	15	1.5		1.5		1.3
Sudan		26		7	57	5.7	8.2	20.3	28.2	
Tanzania	5		25		32	3.2				
Togo		n.a.		n.a.	11	1.1		n.a.	n.a.	n.a.
Tunisia		2		21	35	3.5	1.5			17.5
Uganda		n.a.		n.a.	30	3.0		n.a.	n.a.	n.a.
Upper Volta		n.a.		n.a.	8	.8		n.a.	n.a.	n.a.
Zambia		n.a.		n.a.	50	5.0		n.a.	n.a.	n.a.
Subtotal: Other Africa — 34	**198**	**111**	**131**	**102**	**869**	**86.9**	**226.3**	**91.7**	**144.3**	**67.7**
Grand Total: 106[c]	**4,512**	**3,657**	**3,733**	**2,823**	**20,844**	**2,084.4**	**5,257.9**	**2,380.8**	**5,113.6**	**2,182.2**

[a] Has paid only $0.1 million, so presumably would not receive SDR's.
[b] Became a Fund member in mid-1967.
[c] The Five consist of six countries, and The Ten of eleven, because Belgium and and Luxembourg are joined in a customs and currency union.
n.a. Not available
Definitions: *Surplus* is defined here as an increase, *deficit* as a decrease in the country's gross reserves, consisting of gold, reserve position in the Fund, and foreign exchange.
Source: International Monetary Fund, *International Financial Statistics.*

Index

OTHER SUPPLEMENTARY PAPERS PUBLISHED BY CED

To order CED publications please indicate number in column entitled "# Copies Desired." Then mail this order form and check for total amount in envelope to Distribution Division, CED, 477 Madison Ave., New York, 10022.

Order Number   **Copies Desired**

1S . . THE ECONOMICS OF A FREE SOCIETY
William Benton
October, 1944, 20 pages. (20¢)   _____

6S . . THE CHANGING ECONOMIC FUNCTION
OF THE CENTRAL CITY
Raymond Vernon
January, 1959, 92 pages, 14 tables, 8 charts. ($1.25)   _____

7S . . METROPOLIS AGAINST ITSELF
Robert C. Wood
March, 1959, 56 pages. ($1.00)   _____

10S . . DEVELOPING THE "LITTLE" ECONOMIES
Donald R. Gilmore
April, 1960, 160 pages, 20 tables. ($2.00)   _____

11S . . THE EDUCATION OF BUSINESSMEN
Leonard S. Silk
December, 1960, 48 pages, 9 tables. (75¢)   _____

13S . . THE SOURCES OF ECONOMIC GROWTH
IN THE UNITED STATES AND THE ALTERNATIVES BEFORE US
Edward F. Denison
January, 1962, 308 pages, 4 charts, 33 tables. ($4.00)   _____

15S . . FARMING, FARMERS, AND MARKETS
FOR FARM GOODS
Karl A. Fox, Vernon W. Ruttan, Lawrence W. Witt
November, 1962, 190 pages, 16 charts, 46 tables. ($3.00)   _____

16S . . THE COMMUNITY ECONOMIC BASE STUDY
Charles M. Tiebout
December, 1962, 98 pages, 6 charts, 12 tables. ($1.50)   _____

17S . . HOW A REGION GROWS—
AREA DEVELOPMENT IN THE U.S. ECONOMY
Harvey S. Perloff, with Vera W. Dodds
March, 1963, 152 pages, 21 charts, 23 tables. ($2.25)*   _____

18S . . COMMUNITY ECONOMIC DEVELOPMENT EFFORTS:
FIVE CASE STUDIES
W. Paul Brann, V. C. Crisafulli, Donald R. Gilmore,
Jacob J. Kaufman, Halsey R. Jones, Jr., J. W. Milliman,
John H. Nixon, W. G. Pinnell
December, 1964, 352 pages, 47 tables, 14 charts. ($2.75)*   _____

19S . . CRISIS IN WORLD COMMUNISM—
MARXISM IN SEARCH OF EFFICIENCY
Frank O'Brien
January, 1965, 192 pages. ($2.75)*   _____

SEE OTHER SIDE⟶

☐ Please bill me. (Remittance requested for orders under $3.00)
☐ Please send me CED's current publications list.
☐ I should like to know how I might receive all of CED's future publications
by becoming a Participant in the CED Reader-Forum.
* Hard cover edition available. Prices on request.

DATE DUE
